Family,

The First Line Of Government

APOSTLE STEVE LYSTON

Order this book online at www.trafford.com
or email orders@trafford.com

Most Trafford titles are also available at major online book retailers.

Cover Design: Johann D. A. Williams
Editing: Marsha McCormack

Print information available on the last page.

ISBN: 978-1-4907-8335-2 (sc)
ISBN: 978-1-4907-8336-9 (hc)
ISBN: 978-1-4907-8337-6 (e)

Library of Congress Control Number: 2017909899

Trafford rev. 06/27/2017

Trafford PUBLISHING®   www.trafford.com
North America & international
toll-free: 1 888 232 4444 (USA & Canada)
fax: 812 355 4082

THANK YOUS

Special THANK YOU to The Father, The Son and The Holy Spirit!

A Special **THANK YOU** *also to*

The RWOMI Family globally for your steadfast support

*Bishop Dr. Doris Hutchinson for your unwavering
and genuine support, love, and prayers*

DEDICATION

This book is dedicated first to my family—Michelle Lyston, Shevado Lyston, Hannah Lyston, and Joshua Lyston. This is the journey of a lifetime!

This book is further dedicated to

My mother, Ms. Zelma Thomas

My biological family

My Church family; and

My Military family

CONTENTS

Foreword xi
Preface.. xiii
Introduction... xv

FAMILY

Chapter 1:   The Unity of the Family Brings Success 1
Chapter 2:   Family, Ministry, and Finance 8
Chapter 3:   About Marriage and Remarriage.................................... 16
Chapter 4:   God Hates Divorce.. 22
Chapter 5:   Focus on the Family 29
Chapter 6:   Your In-Laws Should Not Be Outlaws 39
Chapter 7:   Prayer to Defeat All Threats and Attacks Against
             the Family.. 42

MEN

Chapter 8:   Men, Walk in Your Authority 47
Chapter 9:   The Nation Needs Fathers.. 54

WOMEN

Chapter 10: Women: Virtuous, Healed, and Transformed for
             Leadership.. 65
Chapter 11: Mothers, Raise the Standard............................. 74

MEN AND WOMEN

Chapter 12: What Men Want, What Women Want............................. 79
Chapter 13: Parents: The First Role Models 89
Chapter 14: God Cares for the Single Parents.................................. 95
Chapter 15: About Dating and Marriage 99
Chapter 16: Our Children—Our Heritage!................................ 107

Chapter 17: Youth of the Nation Arise!..114
Chapter 18: Abortion on Demand..123
Chapter 19: Stand in the Gap for the Next Generation.......................128

REAL TALK ABOUT SEX

Chapter 20: Good Marriage, Good Sex—Blessings from God...........133
Chapter 21: Spice Up Your Sex Life...136
Chapter 22: Are There Sexual Boundaries? 143
Chapter 23: Ten Mistakes Married Couples Shouldn't Make.............150
Chapter 24: The Pain of Cheating..153
Chapter 25: Order in the Church: Sexual Impurity...........................158
Chapter 26: Sexual Impurity Defiles a Nation 162
Chapter 27: Guard Your Heart! God Wants Intimacy!.......................171
Chapter 28: Love: The Most Misquoted, Misused, and
             Misunderstood Word 175
Chapter 29: Healthy Mind, Healthy Living..182
Chapter 30: Why Commit Suicide?...187

ENCOURAGEMENT FOR THE FAMILY

Chapter 31: Back to Core Values..197
Chapter 32: Choices Determine Success..203
Chapter 33: Christians, Walk In Your Authority.................................210
Chapter 34: Your Past Does Not Determine Your Future 217
Chapter 35: The Power of Fasting and Importance of Prayer.............224
Chapter 36: You Can Make it in Hard Times.....................................232
Chapter 37: God's Blessings on the Family 239

Bibliography...241
About the Author...243

FOREWORD

*F*amily, ***The First Line of Government*** is a timely, solutions-driven book that deals with aspects of family that are not often dealt with in such detail and relevance to the daily challenges we face in our families wearing the various hats we do. This book may/will cause its reader to truly take a second look at the importance and significance of the family, particularly as the family relates to the rest of society.

Most, if not, all of our learned habits have their roots in our family environment, and as we grow and maintain or depart from these habits, that in itself has an impact on the society that we influence.

This is an insightful book, and it has the potential to bring change one person at a time, one family at a time. This book is a game changer, and it's about time the game changed for the family.

With all the influences that are negatively impacting the family today and the changes that many seek to make in order to shift from the original and Divine design and blueprint of the family, ***Family, The First Line of Government*** is a refreshing, tell-it-like-it-is handful of mind-renewing, thought-provoking instrument of change.

Pastor Dr. Michelle Lyston
Restoration World Outreach Ministries Inc.

PREFACE

*F*amily, *The First Line of Government*, is a solutions-oriented and straightforward book that looks at the family as one of the three major institutions that govern every nation and determine its success and growth. We all need to become knowledgeable and understand the purpose, value, role, and significance of the Family, especially in relation to the fulfillment of God's purpose on earth.

It further reveals that the family is a strong, powerful, and influential tool with the potential to accomplish great things and bring change. While many countries are singularly focused on economic development to bring about change, the family has been neglected without the realization that breaking down this institution will ultimately lead to the destruction of a nation.

Family, The First Line of Government includes information that I have garnered from years of Marriage and Family Counseling, Divine revelations, and topics I have written on and addressed in several online and printed publications. This book deals with issues that many discussing them from this angle shy away from, and it will help us to understand that no nation can fully rise unless the family is whole.

INTRODUCTION

Many people focus on financial investments and asset acquisition; meanwhile, nations focus on efforts to achieve economic growth and development; most churches focus on salvation or the size of the building and congregation. This book brings the focus back to the key foundational element for true growth and development that affects individuals, communities, and nations—the Family.

It is now a universal thing for the institution of family to be treated as less important than other issues globally when in fact everything starts in or from the family—it is the most important. Modern parenting has failed, and, in particular, many fathers have failed to stand up the way they should. Generally, we are living in a fatherless society, and even the church is feeling the effects of broken families. Everything starts in the home—even racism! Most children today are growing up not knowing true discipline—especially in single-parent homes, where, instead of focusing on his/her parental role, the single mother or father is forced to play the role of two parents! That is why God is now raising up fathers (Malachi 4:5–6) to put back the family in line.

The nation leaders need to make money available to NGOs, Churches, and faith-based organizations to set up training and mentorship programs, especially for the boys who are being neglected by the society, instead of promoting blatant sexuality and immorality. While women and girls must be taken care of in every way, we cannot neglect our boys and men. If you ask many of the boys on the streets where their fathers are, they will tell you that their fathers abandoned them to live with another family! For some, the "dons"/gang leaders became their "fathers" and role models. We must rescue our boys; they are the future heads of families, and if there is no head, the entire body dies and the nation dies! While it seems this is what we are reaping, all hope is not lost, and if we get back to the principal foundation of family and apply the necessary principles, change for the better will come.

FAMILY

CHAPTER 1

THE UNITY OF THE FAMILY BRINGS SUCCESS

For the family to be successful, it is imperative that the family is healed. If the family is not healed and functioning fully, then both the Church Government and the Civil Government will be affected. Generally speaking, the family institution has been broken and divided as a result of a lack of proper leadership/headship. The absence of the fathers has created a vacuum, and division, disappointment, death, and debt have been filling it.

Every nation, instead of focusing on gender issues, should create a Ministry of Government for Family Affairs and have a full-time government minister to head it—one who is married. Their focus would be on adoption, nutrition, and insurance for the family, child maintenance, mentorship, welfare, conflict resolution, low-income homes, pension, national money management training programs, parenting programs, and family planning. We would see major changes in the economy of every nation that would employ this approach.

It is very difficult to achieve economic goals and growth within a nation when the family is broken. Empowering the family must be the number-one priority. The institution of marriage is being broken, while common-law relationships are increasing and highly promoted; this negatively affects the economy of a nation. We must get on the path to eliminate the promotion of common-law relationships and promote marriage again. Common-law relationships entertain a bastard curse, which negatively affects the nation. Having a sound education is one key element for anyone to have before considering having a child/children. We need to begin again to teach the roles of mothers and fathers. The responsibility and importance of children honoring their biological and spiritual parents must be encouraged and highly promoted; they must be taught the importance of getting the blessings of their parents and the value and impact that it has on their future.

Fathers must step up in their roles because they are the first man in the lives of their daughters and the first mentor in the lives of their sons. They must teach their children discipline, how to pray, how to be principled, and how to be the best they can be in any sphere they enter. Fathers must begin to decree and declare blessings over the lives of their children daily. They must teach their children how to serve and how to avoid the mistakes their parents made.

The Church and the Family

It is also the responsibility of the church to pray that the family is united and that more couples will begin to enter the kingdom so that stability and purity will return to the family. We need to pray for revival, restoration, and healing to come to the family.

I have observed many times the churches hosting conferences and conventions, but very few are for the family, and the greatest problems that now exist within the Church are broken families and financial issues—even within church leadership. The failure of leadership within the Church is the result of the broken family. The Bible specifically speaks about managing his household properly before management of the house of God. Many leaders within the Church have families that are broken and scattered, and God wants us to be the example that the world will follow.

There needs to be more intercession within the Church for the family. It is time for all stakeholders—the three levels of family—to create laws that will bring positive change within the family. God did not create a divided family. The first man and woman were a microcosm of the Church; hence, blessings and prosperity will come as we function according to the blueprint God set for families.

The enemy of souls hates a Godly family, and only through division of the family can he rob us. Genesis 1:26–28 states: "Then God said, 'Let Us make man in Our image, according to Our likeness; let them have dominion over the fish of the sea, over the birds of the air, and over the cattle, over all the earth and over every creeping thing that creeps on the earth.' So God created man in His *own* image; in the image of God He created him; male and female He created them. Then God blessed them, and God said to them, 'Be fruitful and multiply; fill the earth and subdue it; have dominion over the fish of the sea, over the birds of the air, and over every living thing that moves on the earth.'"

We must rise up and pull down the aggressive satanic forces that are coming against the family. We have the authority to bind and to loose and to tear down every wicked law and every wicked system that seeks to destroy the family. We cannot allow the enemy to take away the authority that God has given us.

Many are pushing self-rule and independence from God, but any rule without God brings chaos, disaster, crime, and violence. Recognize that attacking the family is an attack on the government of the Church and of God. The more man pulls away from God, the more turmoil, trouble, pestilence, perversion, rapes, murders, death, and destruction take place. We see it in the schools and on the streets, and it has the potential to spread even further than we can imagine.

The Cry of the Family

With the economy, the way it stands globally, the family has been the institution that is being displaced and destroyed. While most leaders speak about large investments and economic recovery, very little has been done to help the family. Currently, the institution of family is in shambles. There cannot be economic growth and crime reduction within a nation when the family is literally being wiped out.

For the past seven years, there has been a major decline in several areas of our society—globally and locally—such as in the family, finance, jobs, as well as values and morality! Many more families are homeless, others suffering divorce. Many within various families have been compromising by giving sexual favors to keep their jobs. Prostitution is on the rise. Many more small businesses are being wiped out. Many are losing their estate, and more persons are getting involved in crime.

If the family is the foundation of the society and the first form of government that exists, then for every decision that is made within a nation, the family must be the number-one criterion for the decisions made! It is not fair to criticize even the members of our police force when their own families are in disarray! We come down on them to reduce crime, but their own families are suffering also.

We need more programs to be created to help the family. For example, health programs should be one of many developed to give family life a "kick start" of sorts.

We need laws to protect and preserve the family, not to separate and destroy it. There should be more assistance for tuitions and more skills training centers in the community. Financial counseling should be a mandatory program within communities as well as job loss counseling, debt management programs, and other counseling programs that help those who have had job losses to regain focus and confidence.

We also need more low-income housing opportunities getting into the right hands. There needs to be a three-year tax break for persons to start new businesses.

There needs to be full-fledged nutrition programs for the family— programs to teach families how to access healthy food options and also how to manipulate what they have on hand to make better/healthier meals.

No country should be spending more on roads and security than they are spending to help and maintain a strong and healthy population. Without the families, there is no need for either government or roads or anyone to secure!

When we begin to deal with the needs of the families, then things will begin to change, especially for those at the base. If the feet of the nation are not healthy, the head will be going nowhere!

Healing in the Family

The whole purpose of creation was family!

The whole purpose of a Savior is to redeem the family. There has to be healing of the family before there can be healing of an economy.

If the Church, the political arena and the civic organizations, as well as international financial lenders do not have family-friendly policies and systems in place to better assist the family, then we will see more global catastrophes. Today, people don't have the time to spend with their families anymore as a result of the need for survival.

We can't even choose leaders to lead our society and different sectors unless there are strong family values.

There was once a time where a family could sit around the dining table and learn about each other and grow together. That's where intelligence gathering and counseling would take place, because the family is the first line of government.

We are now seeing policies being put in place under the guise of investment, which are ultimately wiping out the day of worship. Spiritual development is part of family growth, and that has been not only threatened, but also totally disregarded! When we disregard that one day of rest and worship, then a greater problem is being created. We are tearing down the foundation of family.

The time has come that if we want to see change globally and locally, the walls of the institution of family must be rebuilt. Systems must be in place that the families can bond again. Many of the problems that exist today stem from the brokenness within the family institution. This includes persons who are placed in different leadership positions who have come from broken families and have not been healed. As such, it spills over into the society and spreads.

Defending Your Family

We are now living in a time where many people don't value life the way they used to or should. Yet, from time to time, we will hear people say, "How can he be a Christian and he's carrying a gun?" or "How can he be a Pastor and he's carrying a gun?" Some would respond, "That's not right!" However, regardless of whether they are Christian Pastors, Christian soldiers, Christian police, Christian lawyers, Christian anybody—each has a right to carry legal weapons to protect their lives, property, and families.

However, Richard Henry Lee (1732–1794), a signer of the US Declaration of Independence who helped form the Second Amendment in the First Congress, wrote: "To preserve liberty, it is essential that the whole body of people always possess arms and be taught alike." Interestingly, most wealthy people always teach their children at an early age how to use a firearm. There is no scripture in the Bible that says that Christians should not bear arms. While firearms did not exist then, all the people were armed. The book of Nehemiah tells it. They carried bow, spears, swords, slingshots, darts, arrows, and more, for war and self-defense (Nehemiah 4:17–18).

Many times, people will quote the scripture "Thou shalt not kill" when it comes to Christians (Exodus 20:13). The Hebrew word for "kill" in that context is *ratsach,* which, when translated, means "to murder." The *Oxford Illustrated Dictionary* clearly explains the difference between *killing* and *murder. Murder* is the "unlawful, intentional killing of a human being with malice or aforethought." Thus, what the Bible was speaking of was not self-defense but the intention based on the hatred, revenge, and anger fostered in the heart and breeding an evil intention to murder. But if, as a Christian, someone enters your home to rob, murder, or rape you or your family member(s), you have the right to defend yourself, your family, and your property.

A number of persons quote Matthew 5: 38–39 also to justify their actions. However, this scripture was not telling us as Christians to be passive; nor was it instigating violence, murder, and stupidity. The Lord was not telling us that if someone punches us on the left side of our face, we should turn the right side also so they could punch it too! Certainly not! The Lord was telling us that where someone does evil against you, you are to leave vengeance to Him and to the law of the land to deal with it. So we are not to seek or to take revenge ourselves is what He was saying. When someone comes after you with a deliberate evil intention, don't go back after them; at that point, it festers in the heart and becomes revenge, and if you kill them for that, it becomes murder—not self-defense!

Luke 22:35–36 says, "And He said to them, 'When I sent you without money bag, knapsack, and sandals, did you lack anything?' So they said, 'Nothing.' Then He said to them, 'But now, he who has a money bag, let him take it, and likewise a knapsack; and he who has no sword, let him sell his garment and buy one.'"

The Lord was revealing to His disciples—as He is to us today—that the times and state of things would change and even get worse, security-wise and economically! Meeting the needs would not be as it was when He was on earth! So they would need to ensure that they are prepared in the area of security!

Believers also must accept the protection of an ordered government of the land. But the family is also the first line of government. The man as the head is responsible for the physical and spiritual protection of his household (Ephesians 5:25–33).

So as a Christian, would you allow the strongman to come into your house and ravish your family and rob you of your property?

In the same way that the tablet used in the days of old are indeed very different from the tablets we use today; the sword was the number-one weapon of use in battles and self-defense in the days of old. However, today, a sword is outdated and is only used on parade in a military square. They have now upgraded from swords to guns. Things and times have changed. The gun is a more accurate and up-to-date weapon than the sword and the stone.

There is nothing wrong with a Christian using a gun for self-defense. What would be wrong is if the Christian's trust is placed more on the gun than in God! For the Christian, God must always be the first source of protection!

CHAPTER 2

FAMILY, MINISTRY, AND FINANCE

God wants the families to have finances, but God must be first and foremost in our finances. Oftentimes, people will put more effort toward the systems of the world while ignoring Biblical principles when dealing with finances. You will see people trying to pay off their debts, fix their credit, but ignore simple things such as tithing, paying the vows they made to the Lord, or giving firstfruits to the One Who gave them the power to get wealth. True prosperity will only come when we begin to place great value on Spiritual things. Neglecting the things of God allows you to pay dearly in the long run. God wants us to have good credit with Him, not bad credit. There is a coming wealth transfer for God's people, but it is only for those who value His principles. If God can't trust someone with the small things, how will He then entrust them with bigger things?

Many say they love God, and many others will say they believe in the benefits and manifestations of God—healing and miracles. However, when it comes to tithing, giving in any form, they have a problem with that. This is what you call *greed*. If God doesn't have your pocket, then He doesn't control your heart either. Love is about giving. God wants to bless the family to be a unit of lenders.

Changes within the economy of a nation begin in the home (1 Timothy 3:5). The home is where money management takes place and where financial responsibility must first be taught. When we fail to manage financially in the home, it will impact on the nation and on the Church itself.

So financial management, parenting, moral values, proper attitudes, grooming, and etiquette start in the home. When, for example, someone wastes water, energy, and simple things such as toilet paper and food within the home, they will do the same thing elsewhere. This is one of the reasons I say, the state of the nation is a reflection of what is happening in the church and in the family. If we are going to reduce poverty or debt within a nation, we must begin to empower the family. We must teach the children from a tender age about credit and debit, credit cards, money management, and equitable distribution of resources.

Furthermore, we must teach our children about giving God His 10 percent and the benefits of tithing. When we put God first in our finance, He will put us first, too, and give us the necessary strategies and tactics. Tithing gives us a heavenly download to be ahead of the game always. He gives us business ideas and strategies.

We also need to teach our boys from a young age not to be womanizers, not to be disrespectful to women, and not to waste their money on alcohol and gambling—all these things destroy families. Teach our men-in-the-making about honor, submission, discipline, and respect within the home. The most important thing that would help them with their finance is to marry the right person. The right person will help to preserve their legacy. Marrying the wrong person will lead to a waste/squandering of your money and resources. Teach the children self-control if they want to have financial freedom. Not everything a child wants must be given to them. We cannot allow our children to continue to be slaves to international lenders who are corrupting many nations. The family has to be free.

Money, Sex, and the Family

Money and sex are the greatest demands of man today! Most decisions are now being centered on those two areas, and it is now seriously affecting every sector of the society. Many countries and individuals are now lining up to endorse certain activities and lifestyles that are related to money and sex. Who knows if the Anti-Christ won't come through those two areas? Revelation 13:17 says, "And that no one may buy or sell except one who has the mark of the name of the beast, or the number of his name."

Both money and sex were instituted by God, and both are there to give God glory. There is nothing wrong with either, but the action and the motives behind them determine the direction things go—whether good or bad. There is nothing wrong with money itself or being wealthy, but the issue lies in how it was acquired and its source. Those who are wealthy must endeavor to be good stewards and must do good—carry out good work—being willing to share for the benefit of mankind. Wealth should not be used to sponsor and/or promote evil, which destroys the family, perverts the course of justice, promotes the sex trade, human trafficking, adultery, and immorality, and ultimately brings down the fabric of the nation. Sadly, the very persons who should be instituting the proper values and attitudes within the nation are most often the ones who are behind those activities. However, change can come when each person does a self-evaluation and asks himself/herself the question, *Am I contributing to the building or the devaluing of the nation?*

Family, Fight Back

There are many decisions a family has to make for survival. In order to remain together, for example, a family must be willing to stand together against the wrong motives behind money and sex; otherwise, each will need to decide if it is worth it to lose his/her family for money and sex!

Businessmen and politicians, in an effort to gain material things and in pursuit of power and/or wealth, have ruined their families.

Fame, power, wealth, and compromising one's integrity should not be the most important issues in one's life. Anything that you are pursuing more than you are pursuing God, the wholeness of your family life, and the maintenance of your integrity will not only cost you those relationships but also cost you the very things you are pursuing.

People in any capacity (whether in ministry, entertainment industry, or other secular jobs) who travel extensively working locally and/or globally without their partner accompanying them at some point leaves them at great risk. It puts their spousal/familial relationship in jeopardy.

What about a person who spends more time with the secretary or bodyguard or assistant on a daily basis? Does it put that person in a compromising position? Some will say that he/she has to do that to keep food on the table for his/her family. But this compromise can cost him/her that very same family—regardless of the motive. Thus begins the cycle of crime and possible drug use as well as unsupervised children. Every decision that we make must be family oriented, including legislation. Legalizing marijuana will only work against the family, bring greater poverty, increase crime, and negatively affect the education system. What we should be focused on is getting to the root of the matter and seek for the right solutions.

With whom do you communicate with most each day? Is it coworkers, friends, or family?

Family, especially husbands and wives, must encourage each other when times are difficult and things are hard economically. This will make it difficult for those with wrong motives to infiltrate the family and cause damage.

Look for the signals from your family members—statements from your spouse like "We used to go out more" or "You don't dress as nice as you used to." Or when the children say, "We don't go to the beach anymore." Or when they ask, "Daddy/Mummy, what time are you coming home today?" Sometimes when the children's grades start falling or they become rebellious, that is a signal to us that we need to pay closer attention.

- What if family life improved in this way? Would there be a difference in the nation?

- What if the media took a different approach and promoted more family-oriented programs? Would there be a difference in the nation?
- What if every company and the government cut unnecessary spending and redirected those funds to more family-centric activities? Would there be a difference in the nation?
- What if we cut the security costs and channel more to the family-oriented activities? Would there be a difference in the nation?
- What if the banks cut some of their charges that bring a strain on the family? Would there be a difference in the nation?

There are several key points that, when implemented, will positively contribute to the growth of every family:

- Every family must have/make a budget.
- Every family should have proper record-keeping and a place where they can file their bills.
- Avoid late payments to attract interest.
- Scrutinize your invoices when you get them in the mail and keep tabs on consumption.
- Avoid wasting food and try to buy in bulk as much as possible.
- Where your resources can't stretch, avoid popular (more expensive) brands.

These could save you a bundle!

Family and Ministry

One of the most beautiful things that can ever happen is to have family operating in ministry together—husband, wife, and children. Oftentimes, after two people get married, different people and even the media will say that the ministry/the church destroys the family. As a result, many tend to withdraw or hold back on their ministry work in which they were once vibrant and full of zeal. Surprisingly, many spend hours within the secular fields, working even two or three jobs, and never have a problem doing that without realizing that such a routine is destroying their family life and robbing them of the time that could be spent together learning about and growing with each other.

Those who are called to Ministry are those who are in the business of helping, similar to a doctor or a waste management engineer—it is an essential service. There is no more honorable job than to help people and to see lives change. Saving souls and empowering people give joy.

Ministry can be very demanding when you don't have a balanced life. Balance in life is key—time management and being connected to God. When you have a strong relationship with God, He will give you the wisdom, knowledge, understanding, tactics, and strategies on how to function in ministry. Even Jesus at times, in His earthly ministry, would pull away to commune with His Father and ensure that there is no stress or warfare that will be so overwhelming that we can't continue.

When persons get married, it is

- to fulfill God's purpose;
- for child-bearing;
- for the intimacy and companionship, which draw them closer; and
- for God to establish covenants through them.

When a marriage takes place, if they are not connected to the Holy Spirit when they feel overwhelmed, the enemy can deceive them that it is the ministry taking a toll on them, while the enemy remains silent regarding the secular work that eats up their time and relationship.

- Ministry will get overwhelming when there are no boundaries set.
- Uninterrupted time with God. Many people in ministry don't utilize Godly wisdom, for example, by not pulling away uninterrupted, and that indicates that they have no order in their lives.
- Vacation. When it comes to vacation, they take one but are still executing the workload they supposedly left behind.
- Family time. No boundaries are set for family time so that even when they are eating dinner, they are still taking calls ministering to people.

We all need to remember that we are not called to everybody. Neither are we called to save the world. Jesus is the Savior of the World, not us. When tiredness and lack of energy begin to step in so that it starts to affect even your sex life, it means that your marriage is under stress or spiritual warfare. If you have to wait on your energy to return, then you are doing something wrong. It means you are trying to do the work of the Holy Spirit. That exposes us to satanic attacks and other attacks on the family. It means that we have to delegate activities and we have to say no to some things.

Many often want to blame ministry when something is going wrong, but if you are connected to God, ministry does not destroy your family. The world is what destroys your family.

In ministry, there are times we must learn to say no. God wants people to be in ministry, because it is through ministry that He wants to bless us. Working for the world pulls you away from God and hurts us spiritually. Surprisingly, most of those who criticize that ministry is destroying their family, when they pull away and their purpose goes down, their family goes down anyway. How does that show that it was ministry that was doing the damage? But when we put God first (Matthew 6:33), God will give us power to get wealth. He will bless us with businesses (Isaiah 50) that teach us to make profit. He will also release scholarships to our children.

The devil doesn't want people to do ministry, and that is why it is so strenuous on the 5 percent who are faithful and are touching the lives of others. So as soon as God starts to bless people, especially after they are married, the enemy will allow them to focus on material things or they allow the union to become their idol. So each person needs to ask the question, "Why did God put the union together in the first place?" What about the prayer that they prayed before saying that they want to work for God even after marriage? God holds us responsible for every vow that we make.

Many times, when persons get married, one of the spouses or an external influence will try to convince one or both spouses that doing ministry is the wrong choice. So as a result, they pull away from ministry. Most fall away in apostasy while trying to gain through the world's systems without realizing that God is the One Who is our Source.

Another thing that tends to happen is in the area of submission. Some believe that submission asks one party to pull away from their church family or their biological family and that they should no longer associate themselves with family or reach out for help. This has isolated many and has caused many marriages to break up. Submission must be in line with God's Word. Even as the man is the head of the family, there should be no manipulation or twisting of the Word and nothing that would be in violation of God's Word. As we see with Ananias and Sapphira, husband and wife should never conspire together to rob God. Neither husband nor wife should partake in the sin of the other as was the case with Adam and Eve. God must be first in our lives and in our marriages and not another person, thing, or circumstance.

CHAPTER 3

ABOUT MARRIAGE AND REMARRIAGE

A Question Asked About Marriage

A gentleman in search of truth asked me this question once: "Very often I hear people say they are praying for a wife or a husband. I would like someone to educate me on how this is possible. When God made the man and woman, He said, for this cause shall a man leave his mother and father and cling to his own wife, not pray for a wife. I have also encountered persons who declared that God answered their prayers and gave them a partner who later left the marriage. As far as my memory goes, only once has God intervened; He told Joseph, who was engaged to Mary, to not be afraid to make her his wife. Please, I am not trying to ridicule the practice. I need to understand how this works . . . Educate me in this theology, please do so, and I thank you very much."

And after having sought the Lord on it, this was my response to him: "If we look at Genesis, the first thing you will realize is that there was a search for one comparable to him (Adam). Notice also that God did not give Adam the choice of a wife, but He put him in deep sleep (we could call that the first surgery and administration of anesthetics), pulled a rib from him, and created his helpmeet for him—one who was comparable and the right fit!

Oftentimes, people pray, but they refuse God's choice for them. Looks, education, shape, height, and color mean nothing to God. What God is looking for is purpose being fulfilled, and God has a person who is the right fit for each of us. A Lada part will not work effectively in BMW. So we need God to guide us to the right "fit"!

The Word of God says in Proverbs 18:22, "He who finds a wife finds a good thing, and obtains favor from the Lord." So finding does not necessarily mean physically going in search of at all times; praying is part of seeking to find. So in praying, we are seeking God's direction to find, and to find His perfect purpose for us! Furthermore, it is the man who must do the finding, not the woman.

The next thing is that you can find the perfect person but mess up in the "leave and cleave" aspect of things! Leaving and cleaving is more spiritual than physical! We have to leave some friends, ways, families, ideologies behind and give priority what God wants of and in your marriage relationship. Oftentimes, people don't want to do that, so there is ultimately breakdown in communication, and divorce results!

Recognize that man and woman are made differently, so once one refuses the process of "leaving and cleaving," and if their relationship with God is not strong, then he/she will not fully understand

1) himself/herself according to God's purpose for them being together; and

2) what God wants to do with them as a unit. God holds the men more accountable than the women for the family or marriage breakdown because the man is the one God has charged to find, to shelter, to cover, and to feed his wife with the Word of God to deal with any pitfalls or character flaws (Ephesians 5).

So each time a man finds a fault, God first looks at him (the man) and that it is symbolic of the man's relationship with Him. So if a man's wife is stubborn and rebellious, it may be that the husband is as stubborn and rebellious to God and does not want to change.

It is sad to say that a lot of people pray and get God's perfect will for their lives, but they end up losing it because they refuse to obey God's voice or instructions on a daily basis. We only can understand each other through the eyes of God. And when God is not within a marriage, it always breaks down—even if it is God's choice. We have the responsibility of maintaining that favor and gift.

Questions on Marriage, Divorce, and Remarriage

On another occasion, a woman sent me several questions on the issues of Marriage, Divorce, and Remarriage that she wanted answered. Here are the questions she asked and my responses:

"Some churches have strict stance when it comes to the matter of divorce. The thing is that even if women are revealing that their husbands are abusing them, they are still encouraged to 'stay and work it out.' For others, once the person has been divorced, that ends their chance of happiness with another partner, as the church does not support remarriage."

Q: What are the things to consider before going into a marriage?

A: Before marriage takes place, the man must first carefully and prayerfully seek God to determine if this is the person that the Lord wants him to marry. It is the man who does the seeking, not the woman. The woman's role is to prayerfully seek the Lord for the confirmation that it is God's will and that it is also in line with the fulfillment of her purpose. Age and education are not the criteria for whom to marry.

The potential bride has to ensure that her parents play a role in the selection, confirmation, and releasing of the blessing. Scripturally, they must get the blessing of the parents upon the union. Without the blessing of the parents, there is potential for problems down the road.

The man must understand that it is not about his choice; it's about God's choice. God made the choice for Adam. While some may argue that there was only one to choose from, it was God who made whom Adam needed. So the man must trust God to make him the wife He needs for the fulfillment of purpose.

The man has to consider timing. Timing is important. He needs to identify if he has reached that stage of maturity to take on a wife and the leadership of a family. The woman also must take into consideration the requirements of being a wife. She becomes a wife—by principles, willingness to embrace submission and motherhood—before she actually walks in that role! She has to give up her will to embrace and accept God's will and purpose for them both. She must be ready to walk with him through the possibly painful period of leaving and cleaving. That process can be very painful for both, as they are going to leave friends, family, and more to start a life together and away from the familiar territory. Most of all, what if there are differences concerning the issue of children—who wants and who doesn't, and how many, and when? What if he wants sex every night and you don't, or vice versa?

Q: After adhering to all these and it still falls apart . . . what is the basis for throwing in the towel on a marriage?

A: Marriages tend to fall apart when one of the parties is unwilling to change. Poor (or lack of) communication and external family issues play significant roles in the falling apart of a marriage. Money and career are also factors that can negatively affect the success of a marriage. Prosperity can also do this. Both must necessarily keep in mind that their marriage is their greatest investment, and it is even greater than a house or vehicle. Ongoing counseling, prayer, and fasting—every method must first be tried to avert divorce. Marriage is about sacrifices, and God hates divorce. Most marriages fall apart because one party is not following instructions given by Spirit-filled counselors. For example, before a marriage takes place (as in the first question), the Spiritual counselor should discern the issues and the baggage and garbage that each has, and sometimes one has to wait and be healed before continuing to move on to the next relationship. Changing partners does not necessarily mean that the problem has been addressed/solved. They each *must* look and see what their own pitfalls were and how those contributed to the breaking up of the marriage. As human beings, we all tend to point fingers but fail to look at ourselves. In our minds, it is never us; it is always the other person. Hence, the problem remains. Biblically, the only reasons for "throwing in the towel" are as follows:

- physical abuse—so much so that the law of the land has to be involved. Although the Bible is not absolute on it (1 Timothy 3:1–3) *then*, divorce may be an option.
- adultery (Matthew 5)
- faith (1 Corinthians 7:14–16)

When one spouse is not Christian and that spouse willfully and permanently divorces the Christian spouse (1 Corinthians 7:15), then remarriage can take place. When one's mate is guilty of sexual immorality and is unwilling to repent (Matthew 19:8–9), they can remarry.

While the Bible clearly outlines the various things that can cause or allow for divorce, it is the responsibility of the couple to decide if they will go through with it. God can still honor you if you decide to stay and rebuild your marriage. God says in His word that He hates divorce.

Q: What's wrong with that person seeking happiness with someone else?

A: Seeking God's will is more important than "seeking happiness," because once you are in the will of God, automatically, everything else, including your happiness, will follow suit (Matthew 6:33). Happiness is only on the surface and is a matter of satisfying a surface-level desire. Joy is spiritual and much deeper than happiness, and it can only come through Jesus Christ. Likewise, having sex and orgasms are momentary. Life goes on after the moment. God wants to give us a lifelong joy and pleasure beyond what we can imagine. Everything has to be exhausted before throwing in the proverbial towel.

Q: Some churches use scripture to support not remarrying—[please] address this.

A: We can't come against any church and their belief or doctrine. Each church may interpret the Bible in a different way. The right thing to do when there is conflict is to seek the Holy Spirit. But what if you are going to a church that does not believe in the Holy Spirit or that God still speaks to people? If that church adheres directly to word of God, and you have exhausted all channels and divorce is the only option you face and the Lord moves you to remarry, then that person is going to have to get released from that church/denomination and find one that his/her doctrinal beliefs allow for remarriage after divorce.

Q: Any other thought on the matter?

A:

- Remember the marriage vows that are made, and recognize that these vows are taken by faith, for we don't truly know what "better or worse" really is! When the words "in sickness and in health" are said, no one really knows how sick sickness is. We do it not knowing the full extent of what we say but choose to believe.
- Ensure it is God's will for you to remarry someone else.
- Consider the effect it will have on the children and deal with it wisely.
- Also consider attorney fees and assets, and ask yourself if you are willing to walk away from everything and start over.
- Consider if you are ready to deal with the mental and emotional toll that divorce will undoubtedly take on you.
- Are you willing to wait for a period to be healed before you start over?
- Are you willing to fast and pray as exemplified in the movie *War Room*?
- If the person you are divorcing makes a 180-degree turn and changes overnight and then seeks to reenter your life in that way, would you do it?

CHAPTER 4

GOD HATES DIVORCE

*T*he *Gleaner* (Jamaica) recently reported on the high level of divorce within the nation of Jamaica. Recognize that the divorce rates of a nation reflect the spiritual and natural state of the nation.

The family is the first line of government, and if the family is failing, then that explains why the political leadership is failing also. Both the church and the people of the nation should use this information as the catalyst in their determination to rebuild families within the nation. The economy ought not to be the sole focus of rebuilding a nation. When you focus on building families, you are equipping them to make right choices. Making right choices is the center of economics! Everyone is talking about the economy while families are being destroyed, not realizing that without the families, there will be failed economies!

Malachi 2:16 specifically states that God hates divorce. It affects every fiber of a nation—it increases crime and pollutes one's spirit! Divorce brings a negative impact on a nation and even produces unholy seeds!

From a national standpoint, much of the attacks against families stem from decisions made by political leaders, church leaders, and the private sector, including gambling, legalization of certain narcotic drugs, decisions on sex education, flexi-week implementation, divestment, and poor management. The global media are also contributors to the breakdown in marriages—everything is X-rated, and it is right in view of our children and the people.

On a personal level, there is the need to take a good look at communication. Good communication is the key to sustaining a marriage. One must try to be a friend first before there can be a healthy marriage.

In addition to all this, the integration of varying cultures plays a role in many of the misunderstandings that take place in marriages of this nature. For example, in parts of the Middle East and Africa, marriages are held in higher esteem and treated with greater respect than in the West. They usually seek their leader to know if the person is the one God wills for their life. Additionally, each spouse knows his/her role, and there is no competition regarding submission. Even more so, something as simple as parents having to give the blessings before any marriage can take place is honored. Choosing the Best Man/Maid of Honor has nothing to do with friendships but everything to do with mentors and role models—thus, a married couple with strong values and a good marriage is selected to stand with the couple to be married as their Best Couple. After the marriage, the Best Couple would be their first line of counseling if needed.

Here in the West, the attitude is "if I feel I love you and want to marry you, nothing else matters." That is not the Biblical way. The Biblical way is that God chooses the person; they both seek the Lord to see if that is the person He has ordained. Then God puts it within the spirit of the man, and he will approach her and her family. Then after approval of her parents and his, then negotiations and counseling will take place. Take note that it is the man who must do the pursuing, not the woman! The woman gives the confirmation. The man's decision must be based on God's instructions and choices, not what he feels or her looks or name! If the man gets the wrong "rib," then there will always be issues, and many wrong choices will be made.

Each person must know their role within the marriage. The man is the prophet, king, and priest of the home. So he has to make intercession for his family daily, feed, nourish, and cherish her with the spiritual food.

He has to rule with integrity and holiness as a king and prophesy good things over his wife on a daily basis, meanwhile protecting her from the onslaught of the enemy (Ephesians 5). He is given the authority to name things and to bless (Genesis 2:18–24).

The wife is the helper—meaning, she is his strength for all he is called to be and to do. This is not the "you only stay at home and cook and clean" helper. This is the helper that is positioned with him so that both can fulfill a greater purpose as one! Adam/Man alone was inadequate. The wife complemented him in all that he was called to do. He needed help in his daily work, procreation, support, companionship, and even in spending his money!

Marriage comes with favor! When the marriage is terminated, that favor goes! Fight for your family!

As the saying goes, "Marriage is made in Heaven," but we have to live it on earth! It is an investment that is more valuable than your physical assets!

A Godly wife is favor from God! So every husband who has a Godly wife must realize and appreciate that this is favor from God. It is imperative for husband and wife to speak to each other, while remembering that Proverbs 18:21 states that "Death and life are in the power of the tongue." It is easy to speak negatively in times of disagreement and conflict and more difficult to speak positively. Whatever you call the person negatively, that is what they will become to you. Thus, if the husband calls his wife a Jezebel, then she becomes that to him, and he in turn becomes the Ahab!

Leaving and cleaving is always difficult within a marriage! Becoming one flesh is not easy. This brings about priority changes on the part of the husband/man. There are so many things that they both must leave in order to cleave to each other and become one—family, friends, exes, attitudes, activities, and mind-set. Although God spoke to the man, both man and wife must do this to become one in Him.

Being joined as one has the idea of both passion and preeminence. The term "one flesh" carries a number of implications—sexual union, child conception, spiritual and emotional intimacy, and showing each other the same respect shown to other close kin. Some people show more respect to their friends and relatives than to their spouse.

The first thing a man must realize is that he must see himself in the person who is his wife, because she would complete him! So they will now have one goal, one vision, one set of objectives, and both of them will go after the same thing. They will have the same heart! Their coming together should never be about money, assets, title, fame, or any such thing. It should be about fulfilling purpose and conforming to God's image (Deuteronomy 6:4).

The wife must know that regardless of what is being taught about the role of women, they must know that women were made for men, not men for women (1 Corinthians 11:9). Submission is not an act of weakness; it is an act of purpose and protection.

Man was first created—meaning that priority and responsibility were given to the man by God as head of the family. It means he is held accountable for his family! He must rule lovingly and gently. Creation's origin lets us know that man was created from the dust and woman from the rib of man (1 Corinthians 11:8).

Further to this, it is Man who named Woman and all other living things (Genesis 1:28; Genesis 2:19; Genesis 2:23). Delegation principle—God gave instructions to Adam on how to manage (Genesis 2:16–18). Woman sinned first (1 Timothy 2:14; Genesis 3:1). However, although it was Eve who first sinned, it was Adam that God held accountable for her actions, for it was Adam that God gave the responsibility to nourish his wife with the instructions of God and relay to her all that God required of them as a union.

Man is the glory of God; woman is the glory of a man (1 Corinthians 11:7). A good woman and a Godly one is not afraid to submit (1 Peter 3:5–6), and there is no shame in that.

The Danger of Divorce

Divorce is dangerous to society! When divorce starts increasing, everyone should be alarmed, including the lawmakers. There are two scriptural grounds given for divorce—sexual immorality and desertion (Matthew 5:32; 1 Corinthians 7:1–6).

Many divorces are taking place without Scriptural grounds, and while it may seem OK to some by way of the courts to grant divorces/ annulments of marriages, there are Spiritual consequences that are taking place. There is a great deal of spiritual polygamy taking place today. Malachi 2:15–16 speaks about the dangers of allowing one's spirit to be corrupted that one would deal treacherously with the wife of one's *youth*.

When two people marry, God stands as a witness to the marriage, sealing it with the strongest possible word—covenant! *Covenant is extremely important to God* and speaks of faithfulness and enduring commitment.

Divorce is considered by God to be "violence" against God's intention for marriage! It is contrary to God's original institution, and in effect, it constitutes an attack on the sacredness of the home and the family unit, which was prescribed by God in the Garden of Eden. Furthermore, whoever divorces his wife for any reason than sexual immorality causes her to commit adultery.

Family, Divorce, and the Economy

Family is the main underpinning element in the stability and growth of a nation. Without a proper familial structure within any nation, instability begins to eat away at many other facets in the society including the economy.

When families struggle in any way, marriages come under a tremendous strain, which affects their ability to perform well on their jobs! So productivity declines. When a divorce ensues, the finances that would normally come into the family home are further depleted as legal, and other administrative costs are added to the equation. Furthermore, the division of the family negatively affects the children, and their studies/productivity are affected. Oftentimes, these children turn to crime. Emotional and mental damage is done to all parties involved. In addition to that, domestic violence and other related crimes will increase, which will pull on the already strained resources of the police force, emergency services, courts/judicial system, health sector, and so many other areas that we may not readily see. Ultimately, the economy is negatively affected and, in turn, negatively affects families and marriages as pressures mount!

Although there are statistics to show the various levels of the divorce rates, we must recognize that the numbers represent real families that are being torn apart and broken up, causing great pain to the children, hurt and heartache for the spouses, and jobs that will not get the full attention required because of the turmoil it causes those involved.

Economic Factors Affecting the Family

The present global economic situation is forcing many couples to engage in the wrong activities to survive—infidelity, long hours with low pay, and, from the other end of the scale, the introduction of the flexi-week where job functions continue all seven days of the week; in some cases, some persons work seven days to survive. As a result of this, families are neglected, schoolwork is affected because of the absence of the parents, and there is no spiritual building up, refreshing, or growth taking place. Even God rested!

So companies—even the essential services—need to introduce staggered shifts. This saves jobs, cuts cost, and helps the families!

We must ensure that we do not introduce any system that will help to pull families apart and cause a spiritual bankruptcy, which ultimately leads to natural bankruptcy!

The economy will soon bounce back, not because of the political and economic "fixes" but because of the cry of the family!

Immigration Reforms

This is a worldwide issue where the policies are helping to destroy families. There needs to be reforms for quicker processing. In seeking to produce better for their families, husbands and wives grow apart; children become estranged and channel their energies to violent behavior. This also affects the children's education.

If countries should make reforms with the welfare of families as their number-one priority, there would be great success and blessings on those administrations. The United States should lead the way!

Personal Communications and Social Networking

Social networking takes up a big chunk of our lives and lifestyle and has become the norm. Sadly, it is eroding personal communication within marriages and familial relationships—so much so that our children are more at ease texting each other rather than spending time face-to-face getting to know each other.

Social networking can be lethal to a marriage relationship if it is not properly and responsibly managed, and there must be the realization that social networking cannot replace quality relationships; nor can it truly replace the value of face-to-face/person-to-person connections.

One thing that many don't realize is that once marriage sharing takes the place of privacy. So something as simple as a password to your e-mail and social network sites should not be private. Persons are afraid to do away with things from past relationships.

Financial Freedom

The family must unite and pray for specific ways for their needs to be met. For example, pray for a business or for business ideas. Oftentimes, long hours don't add to income; it just increases debt!

Family is important, and certain blessings will not come to a nation and its people if the family is unstable or broken!

CHAPTER 5

FOCUS ON THE FAMILY

Many negative things have been coming against the family. Unjust laws, bad management, financial hardship, and even the economic meltdown that has been taking place since 2007 have caused the family to suffer many hardships and lose homes among other things. Large companies were bailed out, while the civil government and businesses turned a blind eye on even assisting families to save their homes or even get a modification on their mortgages. Banks were at the ready to get the homes that ultimately lay rotting away. Some of those homes were pawned to friends for very little more than pocket change, while homelessness increased and families suffered. As a result of all this, some persons committed suicide, some became ill and died, and others are still trying to payoff hospital bills as a result of deteriorated health—thanks to the oppression they faced. Every category of organization—the church, civil society, and businesses—must prioritize the family, particularly when planning, budgeting, and making strategic decisions. Most prioritize other things—machinery, buildings, and so on—while ignoring the family, and when the family is broken, those organizations, communities, and ultimately the nation are broken. As a result, the family, as it stands today, needs healing.

Many organizations that could have offered assistance were more focused on giving millions to promote sexual rights. We are now in a crisis where our boys have been and are being neglected and our fathers have abandoned their homes and families. We have to get back to basics where our focus is on the family. Even the church has lost the mandate that was given by Jesus to set the captives free (Luke 4:18–19). They are more focused on building buildings, not building people.

There are many things that need to be done to rebuild the family. We must get back to basics where we teach our children how to love, how to give, and how to serve, and we must get back to setting up the dinner table again. All stakeholders need to begin putting funding in place and make it available for training and mentorship programs that benefit the family. The government needs to build more low-income homes for families. Companies need to give grants for this purpose also. The older ones within the church begin to teach the younger ones how to be good mothers and fathers before what is taking place now becomes the norm. Fathers need to bless their children, and mothers need to speak positive words over their children on a daily basis. The protocol needs to be reestablished where parents must give the blessings before certain decisions such as getting married take place. We also need to begin hugging our children again, teaching the family to pray and have a sacred place in our home where the family meets and can pray together. There must be affordable health care for families. More food banks need to be set up to help families. If more sports complexes, community centers, and parks in and/or around the various communities, then it will allow the gifts and talents of the youth to be harnessed and developed. The government also needs to work more closely with churches to take care of the spiritual needs of the members of the communities. When we carry out these actions, we reduce crime and violence within the communities. Furthermore, it will reduce the opportunities for dons/gang leaders to become the role models for the young minds. There will also be a reduction in the need to build more prisons.

Fight for the Family

Nehemiah 4:14 says, "And I looked, and arose and said to the nobles, to the leaders, and to the rest of the people, 'Do not be afraid of them. Remember the Lord, great and awesome, and fight for your brethren, your sons, your daughters, your wives, and your houses.'"

The problem that the western countries face, particularly the United States of America, is the breaking down of the wall. While every nation has the responsibility of securing its borders and to protect it from those who want to do harm, recognize that it is not illegal immigrants that are destroying the western countries, especially the USA; it is the rich organizations, Hollywood, and the influence of music, movies, and video games. The infiltration of the Church and the watering down of the Gospel leave us focusing on prosperity, a false prosperity gospel, and we have allowed the enemy to break down the walls.

The wall on which President Trump must focus is the one that rebuilds the family. We have allowed the system to become broken and have removed prayer from the school, communities, and city halls as well as from the workplace and the police force. True light has been removed from the schools and communities while it is being replaced by darkness. Now we are seeing the manifestation of darkness, and it is taking over the nation, while many ignore the root of the problem and we try to focus on racism and other matters. We must identify the true enemies and uproot them from the communities. We must fight for the family. We must rebuild the walls. We must fight and pray against division, divorce, disunity, debt, discouragement, denial, fatherlessness, bastard curses, barrenness, hopelessness, inequality, and oppression.

The greatest investment is not more cars and houses and a bigger church building; neither is it a heftier bank account. It is the *family!* Many, in gaining wealth, destroy their families and have lost the favor of God. At the end of the day, it is your family who will be with you should adversity strike. Many times I have heard leaders and church people talk about revival. But the greatest revival God wants to bring is the healing and restoration of the family according to Malachi 4:5–6, where children will be restored to their fathers, divorce rates will go down, the Jews will begin to preach the gospel again, husbands and wives will begin to do ministry together, families will sit together beside each other, and guesthouses and casinos will become empty. Children will walk away from the pagan rituals and the tattoos that are overrunning the nations. If you realize, Nehemiah addressed five categories for which to fight: "Your brethren, your sons, your daughters, your wives and your houses." Fight for the family and those under you in your household.

- We must decree Isaiah 43:5–7 and Isaiah 49:14–26. So we must decree and command our families to be loosed and to come forth and fulfill their purpose.
- We must pray that God will save our children.
- Confess the above along with Zechariah 2:5 daily.
- We must walk in Genesis 1:28 and be fruitful, increase, subdue the earth, and rule over the seas, birds of the air, and so on. The enemy daily influences the passing of laws in an effort to destroy the family. We must remember that the covenant God has with Abraham (Genesis 12:45; Genesis 17:12–13) applies to us also. Every single person connected to us is a member of our household. Remember also the fifth and the seventh commandments because they are critical to the family.

Family Goes Beyond Bloodlines

The moment you become part of Christ, you become part of the big family. The way Christians treat others is surprising. Growing up, I used to hear a song that said, "I'm so glad that I'm a part of the family of God . . ." Nowadays, the greatest fight and attacks come from within the family of God. The enemy within is greater than the enemy without (Psalm 55:12–14).

Whether it be spiritual colleagues or relatives, betrayal hinders God's work and purpose. There are many times you may hear people talk about wealth transfer. What has been holding up the wealth transfer are greed and selfishness. God blesses someone to be a blessing to others. Many have a one-sided view of blessings, and that is why many fellowships and alliances don't work; they focus only on them receiving but not them giving back. The book of Acts shows us the unity of the Apostles, disciples, and brethren, and how they unite and share the resources. These days, we are hearing a false doctrine that is unscriptural that you don't *sow down* but you *sow up*! I wonder if Jesus only "sowed up" when He laid His life down for us. We say we are family, yet we withhold from our brothers. There are many holy men of God who may not have the material blessings, but they are blessed Spiritually, and God wants us to complement each other with the blessings He releases to us. They would rather withhold from their fellow man/brother; so while our brothers in Africa, India, and other nations suffer and struggle, they, instead, prefer to spend millions on refurbishing buildings to compete with others of like mind or with the world!

Several scriptures tell us we should give preference to the Household of Faith first. There are also scriptures that say we should even give to those who can't give back to us. There are even scriptures that tell us to extend double honor to those who serve within the household of God.

There are so many in church today who withhold from God by not tithing, yet they say they love their leaders and that we are one family. We should all learn from the book of Acts that this is hypocrisy.

The banks have been seizing church buildings; many church buildings are being foreclosed, and many investments have gone down the proverbial drain. The world is laughing at us while many pastors brag about how many cars, houses, and planes they own. Meanwhile, we were treating our brothers and sisters like burdens. We must remember that while a person may not have cash or assets, he/she may have the blessings of favor and grace on his/her life that, when released, can cause us to have access or cause doors to open for us or even grant change for us that money can't buy—just as it was for Jacob in the midst of his Laban experience. It is extremely important for us all to respect that grace and anointing on someone's life.

Wealth Transfer

One of the greatest wealth transfers is about to take place— Grace and Favor! That means that there is a shifting of the favor from the "withholders" to the ones who are willing. All the local churches need is more of the Holy Spirit. They don't need a celebrity preacher to "pull" people. God's Glory must not be touched!

As family, we don't compete; we complement. When one benefits in a family, there is a potential for members of the family to gain to fulfill their God-given vision and purpose. We don't need envy and jealousy to operate in a family. It robs us of the greater blessing. As the Church, if we are looking for those involved in sexual immorality, witchcraft, and so on, to come and experience the positive and life-changing love of God and become a part of the family of God, we can't win them over unless we practice what we preach. A family that is not united cannot win the battle against the strongman and the strongholds, the territorial spirit(s) that have been destroying nations and families. If we want to know, take a look at your immediate family or church family and you will identify the issues there.

The struggling of the churches, the communities, and the nation is happening because the three levels of government are not united—the family, the Church, and the civil governments. Certain blessings can only come when the family is united. Intercessors spend more time trying to pray for unity when they should be praying for souls. Countries are going down, while politicians are fighting each other—even politicians who are on the same side. People are more interested in taking charge of a pulpit than they are in going out to evangelize and win souls for the Lord.

When you look on the social media on a daily basis, you will see the levels of dishonor and disrespect that will let you know the state of the nation. The state of the nation is a reflection of the church and the instability of the other two levels of government.

When our children are being abused, are being raped, and start dying, this tells us that there is no covering—that it is a wakeup call and that a serious introspection is needed on our part.

It is time for the generations to look into themselves.

Action Needed

Regardless of our field, if the family is not in line, all-around failure will come. Jesus gave His life for the family. We must rebuild the altar. We are too busy trying to make money on a daily basis while ignoring Matthew 6:33.

No robot can replace the family; neither can any other gender created by the legal system. God's order for life cannot by replaced. We must create an environment in the home by inviting God's Presence.

God wants us to create an environment where we seek Him daily (Matthew 6:33). His Presence will bring healing, deliverance, and power to get wealth. We cannot have a successful family without the power of the Holy Spirit. Even Jesus, in Matthew 3:16, Luke 24:49, and Acts 1:8, had to depend on the Holy Spirit. Many are now turning to new age practices because they have rejected the Holy Spirit. So they try to put a Christian angle on Yoga and Transcendental Meditation, which are all against Biblical principles.

The Man as the Head

God created the men as the head of the family, and they need to *be* the head to lead their families. There are many groups trying to lobby laws in different nations to put the men on the back burner rather than as the leader of the family. This is the fruit of the group called feminists. The men should not be deemed only as sperm donors or simply providers. God created men with "balls," so they must make tough decisions and stand up and fight for and along with their families. They have been created to be the prophets, priests, and kings of their household. They must give spiritual guidance and coverage for their household. They have to feed their families with the Word; pray for their families; watch over their families spiritually, as they are the shepherds; be vigilant against intruders, wolves, or hirelings; and watch out for friends or strangers who want to come in and divide their families. Many times the deceiver won't show up until success starts. If the enemy can't beat us, they will try to join us.

- Watch out for those who always come and make promises.
- Watch out for those who try to play one against the other to divide and conquer.
- When conflict arises, be careful in whom you confide. The men are supposed to watch out for those with bad motives coming around their families. There are people that will watch your family over time and try to come in to cause disturbance the moment they see a window of opportunity.
- Keep your children away from social network.
- Watch out for those who always question your decision.
- Tolerate no rebellion within your environment.
- Watch with your children the shows that they watch and listen for the subtle messages.
- Keep abreast of the educational institutions your children attend and the changes that may take place.
- Keep your children away from the Halloween activities and tattooing and some of the video games. Pray against low self-esteem, rejection, and fear that will attack your family.
- Nip any form of racism, classism, or bullying in the bud. Compliment them daily—find something positive with which to encourage them. It is particularly so when they do a good deed.

Ten Commandments for a Happy Family

(Matthew 6:33; Proverbs 31; Proverbs 18:21; Ephesians 4:26)

1) Seek God *first* especially when making financial, family, and other major decisions!
2) Maintain unity within your household and have one vision for the family. Never compete with but complement each other.
3) Come together, even one day each week—for family devotions, giving God thanks for the things He has done for you, both small and big things. Thanksgiving is one of the keys to prosperity, and it opens the doors of opportunity for you.

4) Spend family time together! Your family is your biggest investment—more valuable than your house, your vehicle, or any other asset. Don't forget the parks, the movies, the beaches, and other family-oriented areas and activities.

5) Ensure that you don't allow any third-party intrusion into your family. Communication is key for a healthy family. If communication breaks down, seek Divine, Spiritual help! Never let the sun go down without resolving the issues that are affecting your communication.

6) Declare blessings upon and speak positively about each other. Words are powerful, and positive words cancel out the curses that come at you from the enemy daily.

7) Build your family relationships on trust! Avoid speaking negatively against each other or hiding financial transactions from each other (like secret accounts and so on).

8) Husbands and Wives, pray and ask God to keep your love life vibrant and that you both will satisfy each other.

9) Husbands and Wives, never deny each other of intimacy.

10) Eat healthy foods and exercise regularly.

Here Are Eight Keys for Families

1) Wives, pray to break soul ties of past connections from your husband, cutting him free from the things that hold him back!

2) Husbands, ensure that you wash your wife with the word, ensuring that you read the scriptures and impart unto her to build you up together in Christ.

3) Husbands and Wives, always come in agreement with prayer for the family and for business decision-making.

4) Husbands, do not allow friends, relatives, or coworkers to be closer to you than your wife!

5) Wives, talk to your husbands or talk to God concerning your family—do not allow girlfriends or relatives to become your "trusted advisors"!

6) Wives, submit to your husbands! Husbands, submit to God!
7) Agree and unite in disciplining the children.
8) Invest in your sex life and pray for the Lord to that aspect of your marriage! Do not deny each other!

CHAPTER 6

YOUR IN-LAWS SHOULD NOT BE OUTLAWS

D
ealing with in-laws is not easy for some families. The lack of knowledge of the role of in-laws can bring great problems within the families. Let me be clear: in-laws on both sides should be a blessing to a family. They should not be biased, and they should always give support after a marriage takes place. There are many times a husband may not want his wife to communicate any further with her parents; the opposite is also true. As a result, the spouse will be disrespectful to the parents or family members of their spouse or will try to poison those relationships.

During marriage counseling, it is often said by one spouse that the other spouse's family doesn't like them. They will go as far as saying that they prefer the family of their ex. As a result, there is a great deal of resentment existing in the relationship. Spouses will also resent their spouse's parents or family members because they did not have such parental figures or family relationships growing up. Some will complain that in-laws want to manipulate and control the relationship. They choose to agree only with their child instead of being objective and fair.

It will sometimes occur that one spouse will use the things they learn at home not simply as a guideline but, instead, as an exact expectation for their own household or marriage, and the other spouse may resent that, particularly if that spouse did not grow up in a similar environment. Further to that, some daughters-in-law may resent their fathers-in-law and may even become bitter, because they did not grow up with their natural fathers playing a significant role (if any at all) in their lives. So, oftentimes, the relationship between themselves and their fathers-in-law get to the point of low or no communication.

Every marriage will go through testing, trials, and problems, but good in-laws will rise to the occasion to give good moral, spiritual, financial support and wise counsel in times of crisis. This is exemplified by Moses' father-in-law, Jethro, who gave Moses wise counsel in leadership and delegation. That saved him from spiritual burnout.

The wisdom of good in-laws must not be neglected, as it is far superior, and they are far more experienced in many areas than the couple.

Good in-laws want to see the success and prosperity of the union and the grandchildren that result. Good in-laws don't have any wrong motives of breaking up the relationship or of becoming competition for the relationship. Instead, they see the union as an addition to their family and embrace it as such.

There are many who get married and, after that, cut their spouse off from parents and in-laws. Some don't even allow their spouse to communicate in any way with their own family members, which is extremely painful and should never be tolerated. Some grandparents don't even get to spend time with their grandchildren.

Many will use Genesis 2:24 as an excuse—leave and cleave. However, while leave and cleave can denote a priority change on the husband's part, which include child conception, emotional intimacy, sexual union, and respect, the scripture never says the couple should cut off parents and relatives.

A good in-law will always give space and time for the leaving and cleaving; they know that everything will not be as it was before in that parent-child relationship. Their approach can ultimately make things better or worse in the relationship network. Furthermore, the union should never see them as a burden but as a blessing.

In the scriptures, Ruth received great inheritance because of her in-law who mentored her (Ruth 1:16–18). Honoring parents includes in-laws, and it brings great blessings. Having a good relationship with God will help to improve your relationship with your in-laws. There is no way we should ever see in-laws as burdens; we need to see them as blessings. The parents-in-law have the authority to bring you into great wealth transfer.

CHAPTER 7

PRAYER TO DEFEAT ALL THREATS AND ATTACKS AGAINST THE FAMILY

Prayer is the family's key to demolishing the plans of the enemy. There are many key words that we can use to cancel out Satan's plans against the family. For example, the words *neutralize*, *eliminate*, and *nullify*.

So what do we pray for?

✓ We must pray to neutralize and eliminate all threats against the family. We have to eliminate the strongman and the strongholds.

✓ We must ask the Lord to expose and defeat all double agents in our midst.

✓ We must destabilize the enemy so that the enemy will not mobilize against us. We must nullify all vows made against the family.

✓ We need to ask the Lord to void all counsels and counselors of the enemy that comes against the family.

✓ We also need to ask the Lord to annul every un-Godly covenant and every un-Godly soul tie and contract made against the family.

Prayer to Defeat All Threats and Attacks against the Family

Father, in the name of Jesus, I come to You right now, and I ask You to neutralize all attacks, plots, and plans against my life, my family, my ministry, and my nation in Jesus' name.

Let every plot and trap of the enemy, to bring shame, disgrace, and reproach, become ineffective in Jesus's name. Let every spiritual, legal, and physical plot, plan, or spoken curse coming against my family be neutralized. Neutralize and cancel all debt, sickness, and diseases. I counteract all petitions and plan of the enemy. I neutralize all satanic altars erected against my life, my family, and my church family in Jesus's name. Cancel out any lies or negative agents against our name. Disarm any spirit that comes against my purpose in Jesus' name. Nullify every plot and attack against my children. We negate the effects of all soul ties, sexual curses, witchcraft against our finance and our physical bodies. Cancel every sabotage, ambush, and/or rebellion from human or satanic agents. Offset all debts with heavenly provision. Cancel out any debt that we owe to any organization. Cancel any prophetic declaration from un-Godly authorities intended to bring harm to us or our family or ministry. Let Your favor and blessing flood us each day. Let Your grace and Your provision manifest in our life. Let overflowing blessings and increase be poured out upon us by You each day. Wherever we go, let uncommon blessings be our portion, in Jesus' name. Amen.

MEN

CHAPTER 8

MEN, WALK IN YOUR AUTHORITY

God has given men (the male of the species) the authority to name and even rename things that He formed. Many of the problems that exist are so because the men are not walking in their authority and are not fulfilling the purpose for which they were each created. They have been given a Divine authority to bless and name things (Genesis 2:19), and they are not doing so.

A man in genuine fellowship with God has amazing intelligence, distinct knowledge of speech, and the capacity to connect words to ideas. When righteous men begin to rise up, rename some things that are out of line, speak words of life within the nation and over businesses and family—only then will we see change within politics, the economy, and even within the families of the nation.

God created man, and then He downloaded into man plans and ideas (Genesis 2). Whatever God downloaded into him, then he would name it, and God sanctioned. Men need to rise up and be the backbone God created them to be within the nation.

Let us also take a look at single women in leadership. While many of them do very well in their various fields of endeavor, there is still an incompleteness and imbalance unless that can only come when joined to a man. It helps to give better balance and even greater success. They cannot effectively fulfill their purpose unless there is a man at their side to birth their purpose (Genesis 2:22). If Adam did not name the being God created to complement him, what would she be called? The male-female component brings balance to the family unit, to the communities, and to the nations.

Men Can Create a New Day

If God has given the authority to name and to bless, then men must know the power of their speech. Whatever the sounds or words that dominate the airwaves or the media, they will become the center of the environment. So if we speak hopelessness and destruction, then that we will reap. If we continue to say that there is nothing better out there or that the Church isn't doing anything, then that is what will loom over the communities and nations. What we speak is powerful and carries weight (Proverbs 18:22). But even if our leaders are not the best, we need to start speaking the things that we want them to be for the people.

Since God has given men the privilege to name and to bless, then the men need to begin declaring the right things over the nation and all contained within. Nothing happens until a word is spoken.

Remember, words create, form, shape, encourage, direct, bless, curse, heal, hurt, increase, and multiply (Genesis 1:3–5). Negativity and unclean words are defiling our nation. Words are weapons. Even good leaders hurt, are abused, and ultimately walk away from their very calling because of words! When the speech of our people—and, in particular, of our men—changes, then we will see change begin as well. It was the spoken word that created economy.

Declaring Change to Your Circumstances

- Your circumstances and the mountains that exist within your life or within the nation can be radically removed as you speak over your bills and debt by faith on a daily basis (Matthew 17:20).

- Major things can happen as you lay your hands over your customer listing and speak prosperity. Watch your sales increase.
- Declare positive changes over your bank account on a daily basis by faith and keep going, and you will be amazed at what will take place.
- Speak words of encouragement and declare great things over your children by faith and over the nation, and you will see how the nation can soar out of its current situation.
- Declare that the politicians and the lawmakers will discern clearly before they go into any bilateral agreement and that they will see any dangers pending and thus seek the Lord for direction so that the nation can be protected from those waiting to consume it.

Let us believe that the politicians will unite for the sake of the nation, put their partisan ideals on the back burner, and put the nation and its people first.

What Body Parts Influence Your Decision?

With the various debates globally on politics, in addition to the massacre at the church in Charleston, South Carolina, the nightclub shooting in Orlando, Florida, and other such activities, many questions are coming to the fore, particularly concerning the youth worldwide!

Without a doubt, everything points back to the men—their decisions and their low performance in doing what they were created to do.

When other body parts begin to influence our decision-making and ultimately lead us, then we will have more problems globally than we would care to imagine.

The head is the most important part of the human body; the eyes to see, the ears to hear, and the brain to think and process.

Most families have no head, and when the head is missing, everything becomes lifeless and dead. The head represents leadership, authority, and structure in much the same way as the Godhead (Ephesians 5:22–23). God created a structure—God the Father, Christ our Head, and then male and then female. A man who refuses to submit to Christ has no authority. Many men have been allowing themselves to be seduced by the different body parts, which ultimately perverts the course of justice, destroys the poor, and affects humanity in many negative ways.

It is imperative for us to understand that when the head gets attacked, all the other organs get attacked! The head has the authority to command every other organ to line up in the body. When the head neglects its God-given function, we have serious problems. The head must cease to allow the heart to lead them in their decision-making. At times, the heart can be a source of evil. All evil begins in the heart! (Matthew 15:16–20).

If God wanted the heart to lead, He would have put the brain in the heart. The head has the capacity to say *no!* Men as the head, our very speech must be pure. We have the capacity to bless and to curse—speak things into being.

Men, you cannot allow the pleasures of this world to cause you to abandon your God-given authority! You cannot abandon your family for the lust of this world! The head is the covering of the household, and when there is no covering, then the family is left open to the elements that attack! The family is being ravaged—many children are not being accepted by their fathers. Many of the men are allowing sexuality, sensuality, and physical attractions to influence their decisions! Men must stop allowing their feet to lead them! Men must stop allowing their external sexual reproductive organs to lead them astray and make decisions that will haunt another generation! God made men with "balls," so they need to have some and live up to their responsibilities and to what is expected of them!

When God is going to bless an individual or a nation, He pours oil on the head first, which ultimately flows down to the rest of the body!

Do you realize that a great deal of our daily battles take place in our minds—battles to stay pure, battles to think right and make the right decisions? The enemy always wants to attack the head. Every other organ on or in the body takes instructions from the head. When that doesn't happen, then everything is out of whack! Most of the problems we are going through with the economy and the levels of lawlessness, crime, violence, injustice, and so on, is as a result of the fact that the head is no longer making the decisions using the brain or discerning. As a result of that, a lot of hatred from women and children is the harvest many men reap! Even within the marketplace or political arena, people are now calling for other "body parts" to lead.

Men, you have the authority to bring change. You are to be the prophet, priest, and king of your household. You are to be the provider, protector of your household, which is the first line of government. You cannot continue to abandon your children, neglect and/or abuse your wives, use women, or walk away from your responsibilities. Because of those actions, there is a curse you have created that is affecting over ten generations, creating hopelessness within the society. If any change is going to take place within the society, it must start from the head first!

Physically Strong, Morally Weak

Every strong leader has a weakness, and because strong leaders attract strong adversaries, it is for this reason that they must surround themselves with strong advisors and wise counsel because it can be a deterrent to their vision.

Many times when great leaders fall, whether in Church or in the secular fields, many people will have an outcry. Oftentimes, however, those with the loudest mouths/voices are often the ones who are pushing for a moral-less society.

The word *moral* in this sense means "a person's standards of behavior or beliefs concerning what is and is not acceptable for them to do."

When strong leaders who are morally weak surround themselves with those who also morally weak, they will further weaken the leader, and that is a recipe for disaster. The problem we are facing globally is not about education/academics but in fact about a moral one.

Samson in the Bible was a physically strong leader, but he was morally weak. The very thing that God raised him up to kill is the very thing that blinded him. He could conquer and kill the Philistines, but he could not control his passion. As a result, it affected his vision, mandate, mission, and purpose.

There are many strong leaders within society, but they have now become politically correct. Some are calling black white, and white black!

Some are being blackmailed; meanwhile, some have literally gone into hiding. Strong morals are the keys to success and prosperity.

If the advisors/counselors possess greed and have money without any moral compass, then it is just a matter of time before they sell their leader to the highest bidder. You need to ask yourself the questions:

- In whom do you confide?
- To whom are you telling your secrets?
- With whom are you in covenant?

Know that it is quite likely that some of you are in covenant with some of those who are still in covenant with those who want to destroy you! Your friend may very well be a friend to your enemy.

Every leader should always observe more closely those who are unwilling to close the door to their enemies and they often want you to give your enemies a chance to be heard. Much like Delilah. If a person is willing to sleep with the boss for promotion or money, then it is only a matter of time before he/she does the same thing with your boss' boss. It is critical for every leader—regardless of gender—to ask God to strengthen them on a daily basis. Oftentimes, when people fall or get into problems, they often say, "It is a mistake" or "It just happened."

If you are the boss/leader and have an issue with sex and self-control, someone may just play the role to trap you in many ways including pregnancy. Always remember that people are attracted to power. When you are a strong person on a mission, there are people whom the *enemy* anoints to pull you down—even family members. There are people within society that are not afraid to use their beauty, skills, and charm to bring the strongest man into captivity.

Most global leaders don't make their decisions through prayer or seeking or by doing what is right for the people. But decisions are influenced by those who are also morally weak. From time to time, I have seen where leaders in organizations put away their most loyal and trusted supporters and embrace the enemy—people who weaken them and jeopardize their mission and the mandate.

We cannot be in covenant with the things that we are called to destroy. We must seek to rise above and move beyond the things and even the people that fuel our weaknesses and even see the bigger picture and recognize that in the capacity of a leader, everyone connected to us is affected by our decisions. If one leader betrays another, then don't you think that he will ultimately betray you?

Most leaders like compliments, but always check the motives behind the compliment. Is the motive of the compliment to manipulate or to motivate?

It is imperative that all the strong men within the society that are placed in influential positions begin to lead as they have been created to lead. The men are dropping the baton, and because of that, we now have a broken society, with broken families. People are looking for mentorship; both boys and girls are looking for love. So it is time for men to ask God to strengthen them to overcome their weaknesses and rise up with balanced strength.

CHAPTER 9

THE NATION NEEDS FATHERS

With all the problems the nation is undergoing right now, including the disorder that is evident, it is an indication that there is a national crisis brewing. The nation needs fathers!

The father functions as the priest for the family, and the reason why there are so many problems is that there is an absence of Godly priests in the home instructing the children. If there is going to be any drastic changes in the nation, there has to be the restoration of Godly fathers.

While mothers are extremely important and hold a treasured place in our hearts and homes, a mother cannot do a father's role in its entirety. God's original order was for fathers to lead and walk in Godly authority. Furthermore, we cannot use gender issues to change that fact. The reason women have had to play the dual role of mother and father in the home is that some of the men have forfeited their priesthood, and we are now seeing its effect play out in our nation through the high levels of crime, violence, political tribalism, lack of order, indiscipline, and other social issues.

The foundation on which a father stands determines the success of his family and, in particular, of his children. A father is a teacher, advisor, and counselor. They are responsible for instilling discipline in their children. They tell them the truth and motivate their children. They encourage them and teach them about the power of forgiveness (Ephesians 4:32). They transfer the inheritance blessing in the lives of their children. A simple laying of hands on their children daily while speaking blessings over them can change their circumstances and bring them into the path of success.

The father must pray in the hearing of their children and teach them to pray (1 Samuel 12:23; Ephesians 6:4).

If you want to know why we are in a political crisis, check how many of our national leaders across the sectors

- had good relationships with their fathers;
- were accepted by their fathers; and
- had their fathers' influence throughout their lives;

While this issue is deeply personal and can be a "touchy" issue for many, we must recognize that unless that cycle is broken, then there are serious problems ahead. We need fathers to break the cycle from their children—cycles such as

- Rejection – Many fathers rejected their children even before they were born.
- Hereditary Illnesses – Fathers have a Godly authority to speak healing over their children.
- Rape and Abuse – Too many children are being abused, raped, and killed. Fathers must stand up against that issue.
- Lack of Forgiveness – It is the father who must show love, affection, and approval to their children.

The collapse and failure of marriages and families are as a result of the marriages taking place without the blessing of the fathers. If we study the Bible carefully, marriage should not take place without the blessing of the father. The father is the covering, and as we all know, where there is no roof, we become exposed to the elements—false doctrines, deceptions, and sexual predators!

We may need to do some research on those who are imprisoned and find out how many of them had a father present when they were growing up. We might be surprised at the results. This is not to say that those with both parents present are incapable of doing wrong, but there is significance to having a father present in the lives of their children. Even if we should speak to the most hard-hearted murderer, once you touch the issue of their fathers, they break down.

The lack of effectiveness of some of the church leaders is as a result of the lack of fathers in the church to mentor and motivate sons and daughters to fulfill their purpose. A person can be a Pastor but not a father!

A real father can turn a failing individual—sports personality, student, or husband—into a success just by being a father to them.

If we are going to look at dealing with crime seriously, then we will have to get judges, lawyers, police, and Godly leaders (not necessarily Pastors) who are good fathers, to bring change.

Father: More than a Sperm Donor!

If we are to experience change within the society, there must be a restoration of the fathers! (Malachi 4:5–6) There are many attacks coming after the men/fathers. Many, including the fathers themselves, don't realize that in their capacity as fathers, they stand as a symbol of God (the Father of us all) covering their families. When they are missing in action, then there is no covering on their families, leaving them open to the elements! If we should check, we might find that the number-one root issue behind the high crime rates is the lack of a father.

Now, because of the symbolism of "father," an attack against the fathers is as an attack against God. Many things within the society today are designed to remove the fathers and destroy them: swing clubs, go-go clubs, gambling, lobby groups, feminist groups, secularists, and others.

Every child needs his/her father—for discipline, for mentoring, and for blessing. The father is the one who ought to train his children, bringing them up in the fear and admonition of the God. The father is responsible for providing for the child to be what God wants him to be. He must nourish them tenderly, spiritually, emotionally, and mentally. The father is God's first line of government on the earth, and the family is the first government!

Any disciplining the mother does is an extension of the father's authority in the home—they are one! The husband/father must take leadership in the area of the family, and the wife/mother must be in submission of the father's responsibility, thus remaining covered under the head. Fathers ought *not* to provoke their children to wrath; neither should they overly discipline their children.

It is important to note, fathers: when you are deliberately missing in action from your children's lives, you are in fact provoking them to wrath in that respect because you are robbing them of their covering, their training, and their future! (Colossians 3:20; Proverbs 1:8).

Many children are fatherless! Most now look at a father as just a sperm donor; but a father is more than that! Men should not even engage in selling their sperm.

There are so many good fathers out there who now feel unappreciated and discouraged because they are being thrown in the same cauldron as those who deliberately walk away from their sacred responsibility of fatherhood!

Fatherhood involves more than just monetary support. It involves self-sacrifice and spiritual and emotional support to his children!

Deceptions

Women, be aware of who you are taking on to yourselves as the question of marriage and the possibility of having children come to the fore. Be aware of

- Moral Deceptions – where it is said, "If it feels good, I can do it!"
- Intellectual Deceptions – when an individual believes that his opinion formed by his intellect is equal to or superior to the Word of God!

- Sexual Deceptions – when people reject the God-ordained, monogamous sexual relationship between a man and his wife as the only acceptable sexual relationship

Influencers of Weak Fathers

Many fathers today have abandoned their responsibilities because they are influenced and even threatened by some jealous and heartless women. These women threaten to hold back sex from these fathers or refuse to sign immigration documents for their husband's children; for example, if he continues to take care of his children that are outside of their relationship. Some engage in serious witchcraft to bind or stop them from taking care of the children outside of their relationship!

A good woman encourages her man to take care of his children— which is his responsibility! She recognizes that regardless of the circumstances from which they came, the children are not at fault! The children did not choose to be born!

I encourage all women to let go and encourage the men to take care of their children. I also encourage all mothers who are bitter to see both sides. It is not just the man who is the real problem. I encourage the children not to hate their fathers; nor should they allow anyone to influence them into speaking negatively about their fathers. I encourage all the pastors to speak the truth when it comes to family and not to watch the offering plate. I encourage nations to put laws in place to bring those fathers into accountability that they will take care of their children!

I compliment all the women who stand alone and make every effort to do the job of both parents in raising their children and raising them right! Your reward will be great!

Good Fathers Are Still Around

It is significantly clear that when Fathers' Day comes around, not as much effort and excitement are generated in comparison to Mothers' Day. Not a lot is done to honor the fathers.

The role of a father is so important that regardless of what status they hold, how much money we acquire, what we attain in life, and how much we achieve—everyone deeply desires and, to some extent, needs the love of and relationship with a father.

The state of politics, businesses, and other areas of leadership is as a result of the absence of good fathers in their lives! Many of them have grown up without a father. But most of them were given the family name to hide the "embarrassment." Today, there are even great leaders who are hurt as a result of the absence of their fathers. Paul outlined in 1 Corinthians 15 that there are many instructors but not many fathers.

Good fathers motivate and challenge their children to excel to the highest level. They make the difference in the lives of their children, and this carries a lifelong impact! This was the example set by our Heavenly Father.

Good fathers willingly sacrifice. Again, our Heavenly Father exemplified this action when He sent His Son to lay His life down for us—a sacrifice.

- A good father leaves a legacy for his children (Spiritually or naturally).
- A good father takes time out to listen to his children.
- A good father teaches his children about honor and respect for man and God.
- A good father prays for his children and speaks positively over their lives, even in times of struggle (1 Samuel 12:23; Proverbs 18:22).
- A good father does not compromise and teaches his children the truth.
- A good father knows that the only real truth in this world is in the Bible, and that alone sets the standard for morality and righteousness.
- A good father is serious about whom their children marry because they want to ensure that the legacy remains within the family. They know that if their children marry the wrong person, then that legacy and all the hard work they put in to acquire the

spiritual and physical wealth will be destroyed (Genesis 24:1–5; Deuteronomy 7:3–4).

- A good father works hard to give their children a solid education, even when they themselves don't have one. They will put themselves aside to ensure that their children receive that!

Believe it or not, there are many fathers today who actually do all this!

The father as the head and authority within the family is so important that there are many devices and schemes in this world to get them destabilized, demotivated, and shifted out of position. Once they are shifted out of position, the family is left open to the elements—spiritual, emotional, and even physical brokenness—as a result, gambling, pornography, promiscuity, drug abuse, and anger, among other negative issues, become commonplace and take the front seat, leaving the family to fight without the covering of the father.

The Blessing of a Father

A father's blessing is so important that it can change the destiny of their children. A good father blesses his children publicly and particularly at life-changing points in the lives of their children! (Matthew 3:17; Matthew 17:5; and 2 Peter 1:17–18). They should be there at the christening of their own children and at their children's graduation, baptism, and wedding. They should be present at the birth of each grandchild—as long as they are alive!

Whether spiritually or biologically, most people suffer because they have not received the blessing of their father! The blessings of a father transfer the legacy to his children.

If all the successful fathers begin to speak words of blessings upon their children and the children within the community, especially those who are fatherless, then we will see curses broken, and we will see change. People will begin to fulfill their purpose and walk into their destiny. Some say there needs to be more women in politics, but what is truly needed are more fathers!

There are still good fathers out there, and they need to be celebrated. The focus of a Fathers' Day should not be to promote it less because bad fathers exist but to promote the fathers who *do* stay around and do a good job! There are good fathers who make the sacrifices necessary to see their families succeed and do well! Let them know that they are appreciated and loved, and don't rob them of experiencing that joy—the good ones deserve it!

WOMEN

Chapter 10

WOMEN: VIRTUOUS, HEALED, AND TRANSFORMED FOR LEADERSHIP

Titus 2:3–5 says, "The older women likewise, that they be reverent in behavior, not slanderers, not given to much wine, teachers of good things—that they admonish the young women to love their husbands, to love their children, to be discreet, chaste, homemakers, good, obedient to their own husbands, that the word of God may not be blasphemed."

When someone has a good mother or good mentor, that one must always honor her. Every mother should look on the life of Eve, the first mother. While many may think she is a failure, it was not easy for her because she had no other woman around to teach her or from whom to learn. Women are carriers of good things. There are many scriptures in the Bible that show us how God uses women to make a shift in the earth.

Women always watch over God's word to see it come to pass. God uses women to break traditions. Both men and women are made for different roles and purposes, and we must recognize that women are very important in God's plans. While the enemy may have succeeded in causing the first of the human race to fall, God turned it around and used the woman to birth the Savior. Sometimes what the enemy would use to destroy, God will turn it around and use it to destroy the enemy. God will use women to bring revival in the end-time. It is the older women who are to teach the younger ones so that reproach may not come to the Body of Christ—the Church itself. There is a serious lack of virtuous, spiritually mature women in the Body of Christ. There are very few role models in the Body of Christ and even in the political field who can set proper examples by Biblical standards. Oftentimes, people blame the politicians for the state of our women, but we must go back to basics and ask God to raise up virtuous women. Many women today in positions of authority and decision-making are hurt, suffered abuse, and have become embittered by the experiences they have had but have not yet been healed. Oftentimes, their decisions are fueled by their pain.

Women must be careful whom they choose as their mentors. Their mentor must go beyond merely academic qualifications, popularity, and fame. Their mentors must have a solid foundation that is built on Godly principles. A good mentor will bring success, transformation, and change. There are good mentors mentioned in the Bible such as Naomi. It is critical for women to learn from good, virtuous women to shape their lives.

Needed: Women Who Are Transformed and Healed!

Many are calling for more women in politics and other influential positions within the society, but they must clearly define what kinds of women are needed within those positions. We need women in influential positions who are transformed and healed; or else, we will have chaos within the society.

I have watched many empires and great men fall because of the wrong kind of woman; and if the truth be told, you would be surprised.

There are many distinguished women globally and within the Bible that have contributed to the building of many nations, and we need those women on the frontline. For example, Deborah—a judge whose multiple leadership functions demonstrate the possibility that any woman who will allow God's Spirit to fill their lives will rise to political influence and authority.

Many times you will hear someone call a woman Jezebel, but Jezebel is a spirit that affects hurting women who are not healed and have become cold and wicked. This spirit operates through some women to influence and seduce weak leaders. Jesus speaks of this spirit's characteristics in Revelation 2:23.

Jezebel worships and promotes the Canaanite religion in Israel. It influences people to commit spiritual fornication—meaning, they pull people away from the things of God. They promote immorality; they lobby to bring laws to weaken the church. God will raise up Spirit-filled, transformed, God-fearing women like Deborah—an arbitrator of justice, counselor, wife, wise settler of disputes, deliverer in time of war, and one of great spiritual insight! Furthermore, there will be a great mobilization of people who are gifted in such areas and God-fearing. These are the qualities of women that are being prepared to rebuild nations.

Transformed and Healed

While many organizations and even some arms of the Church fail to utilize women who are healed and transformed in the varying positions, women play some of the greatest roles since the dawn of time. It was women who were the greatest support to Jesus' ministry, and they are, to date, the greatest supporters of the local church. The enemy has been attacking women from the beginning of time, simply because they are an excellent source of positive support! The abuse of our boys, the breaking up of the family, and the reason so many of our men are in prison is a lack of transformed and healed women within our society who understand their roles and responsibilities.

It is the women who train the men in the Bible how men should treat women and how kings should rule (Proverbs 31). They taught their sons what kind of women they should marry. It is the older women who should teach the younger women how to be a wife and how to dress.

The breakdown of our women has created a vacuum and instability globally. There is a conflict that exists between women and the enemy (Genesis 3).

The enemy knows the power and influence women carry, so he tries to create lobby and feminist groups to destroy families.

I believe that unless we quickly reach and empower our women, those who are abused to be healed, then the enemy is going to use women as the number-one terrorist group.

Everything God does, the enemy tries to duplicate or counterfeit, so God is going to bring the greatest transformation and revival through women in the same way that He has used women to bring great justice and wealth transfer. Thus, there are many modern Mordecais, as in the book of Esther, who are mentoring hurting women to be used to bring great changes within nations, and the Hamans that have been lying to kings and giving poor advice, and who have been plotting to kill God's people will be removed.

Healing

The lack of fathers within the home has brought great hurt to many women. Many suffer from rejection, insecurity, lack of confidence, and other emotional problems. Some have turned to the occult seeking help and healing, but only Spiritual healing can bring the change they need. Once they are healed and transformed, they will persuade many, including the men within the society that are found wanting! They will become the true public relations (PR) persons for truth and righteousness within a nation. They will be that voice crying out for the rebuilding of family values within the nation.

Let us all unite and pray that there will be a healing within our women.

Another Question on Marriage

Some churches have a strict stance when it comes to the matter of divorce. For example, women have revealed that their husbands are abusing them, and they are encouraged to "stay and work it out." For others, once the person has been divorced, that ends their opportunity for marital happiness with someone new, as the church they attend does not support remarriage. (See chapter 3.)

Women Need to Be Healed Before They Lead

Last year, the world stage was dominated by women in both negative and positive ways. It was particularly so in the areas of politics and entertainment—both locally and overseas. Many of them were in the news: Miley Cyrus, Lady Saw, D'Angel, Beyoncé, Tessanne Chin, German Chancellor Angela Merkel, Prime Minister of Trinidad and Tobago Kamla Persad-Bissessar, and The Honorable Portia Simpson-Miller. While many believe that women should not be in a place of leadership or even up front—whether in the world or in the Church—it is hypocrisy!

There is nothing wrong with women in leadership; I have worked with excellent female leaders! However, the problem that exists with regard to female leaders in particular is that many of them have been hurt but were not healed.

As human beings, our experiences help to drive our decision–making process. As such, many women have experienced some very difficult and oftentimes painful situations—abuse, infidelity, personal insecurities, rejection, missed opportunities, among other things—and still have the strength to function in their various capacities. Some have insecurities especially with younger ones around. Some may also feel insecure in their capacity to do their job or to keep their family together, which have led some of them to make grave mistakes. There are some women who will behave in the most derogatory ways to get attention. Others will behave extremely aggressive and mean in the office environment, and this negatively affects the environment and can hinder production overall.

Don't Look at the Outward Appearance

Many women will look "tough" on the outside, but, internally, they are fearful and deeply wounded, unable to trust anyone. Some may even resort to alcohol and/or drugs. Some, because of neglect, will just shop endlessly. Some turn to the Church for help.

There is so much potential in our women, and they are valuable in all areas! It is sad that many agents and managers and advisors to many of our women oftentimes build a wall around them, not to protect them but to use them for personal gain.

There is a need for a balanced society, and if we are to get there, then our women need to be healed. In the way of the world, our women are not even given good time to heal after bringing forth another human being into the world.

I have been allowed the opportunity to counsel some of the VIP women, and I have seen the abuse and the suffering they have had to go through on a daily basis while many will demand maximum performance from them. Even journalists, at times, would speak things about them that are not so. The media has hurt many of them because of ignorance.

Even the way in which many of the women in the entertainment industry are attired, it is not their choice or desire at times; and some are forced to do so and are sometimes forced to create an image.

Men, we need to treat our women in the same way we would treat our daughters! Women, value yourselves highly and don't lower your standards. Furthermore, forgive those who have hurt you. Your healing begins with forgiveness.

Men, stand up, protect, and respect your women. Understand that as we function together in our society, a great deal of pressure comes against women to destroy them and their families; so do all you can to protect them where you can. When you commit infidelity, it leaves deep emotional scars and hurts them.

So while the tabloids make a great deal of money on women and their public and private pain, recognize that we have an inherent responsibility to protect the gifts called "Women"!

Some men may believe that satisfying women with money, sex, hype, fame, and a certain lifestyle is all. However, more often than not, what many women desire is to be respected, taken seriously, listened to, and loved!

Women, don't allow the things you have gone through in the past or even on a daily basis isolate you from others or negatively affect your performance and ultimately push away those around you that are good for you and can help to develop the real you!

Draw your strength from God and let your relationship with Him come first! He will direct you on the rest.

Don't use your past to create your future or use it to evaluate others. God wants your inner beauty to shine!

Most of what you have been through, use it as wisdom and use it to help others.

Speak from the heart! Don't allow anyone to create any false personality for you. Be who you are; be healed and come forth!

Virtuous Women Required

One of the reasons there are so many problems eating away at the society is that we are arduously seeking to ensure that individuals achieve academic goals and acquire degrees to excel in their jobs. But very little emphasis is placed on teaching them how to live. The family is the training ground for higher and greater authority. It is the foundation for good governance.

The increase in the levels of child abuse in the nation is a reflection of the general instability of family life, and laws to address this matter are irrelevant. It is going to take more than laws to deal with this issue. We need virtuous women to help to bring balance, which will lead to global change in all sectors.

Proverbs 19:14 reminds us: "Houses and riches *are* an inheritance from fathers, but a prudent wife *is* from the Lord." She increases the family value, estate, and stock—everything!

A contentious wife brings shame, strife, stress, and poverty on her family. She brings the wealth of the family down and depreciates the value of her family. She always looks at things of the past and hinders herself and her family from moving forward. There are women, and there are *virtuous* women!

- A virtuous woman does not fight for headship of the family; she submits to her husband and honors her husband and uses her educational achievements to build up the family. She is not engaged in a battle of the sexes; instead, she understands the functions and purpose of the neck to the body.

- A virtuous woman is always confident and gets involved in her husband's work.
- A virtuous woman is very respectful and does not embarrass her husband or family in public; nor does she tear down her husband with others.
- A virtuous woman gives constructive criticism, and she always sees the potential enemy that would rise up against her family. She sees the fine print. She is the right fit!
- There are too many misfits today, and this causes instability within the families and the nation.
- A virtuous woman sticks with her family at all times—good or bad—and does not abandon her family or dump her husband when she climbs the social ladder or becomes more educated.

Other Characteristics of a Virtuous Woman

A virtuous woman

- always thinks ahead concerning various possibilities that would negatively affect her household and prepares for such things;
- always gets involved in humanitarian efforts—she helps the poor;
- prays for her family, church, and nation, and fears the Lord;
- is respected by her children;
- walks in wisdom and is not idle—she is very industrious;
- is an example wherever she goes and represents her husband and her children very well;
- depends on God for her daily provision and supports the vision of her husband;
- goes for the best in goods and services;
- is multifunctional and carries herself with grace—even under pressure;
- does not nag and pressure her husband but, instead, seeks to come up with solutions to bring balance to her family;

- does not deny her husband of sex even after an argument;
- does not allow influential environments or people to change her values—she changes the environment instead;
- is a mother! She does not have a helper who becomes the mother for her children because she is too busy to find out what is going on in the lives of her children and help deal with it. She does not neglect her children, husband, or their welfare for a mere satisfaction of self. She does not spend hours on the social network, on the phone, or out with girlfriends to the detriment of her marriage and children.
- is a good cook—or is at least willing to learn—and does not depend on fast food.

We need a change now, and the nation needs the virtuous women to rise up, make the difference, and set an example for the next generation.

CHAPTER 11

MOTHERS, RAISE THE STANDARD

Mothers are the neck of the society. The neck is the supporting structure for the father who is the head of the family. The neck is often associated with beauty and a place on which valuables are placed for the entire world to see.

Part of a good mother's role is to nurture their young with milk to the point of maturity. She shapes their lives and instills values and morals within the children in preparation for their future and that of the society. Every good mother knows that such nurturing begins in the womb, and that during breastfeeding, there is a special bonding that takes place between child and mother that is irreplaceable and unique to each child.

We are in a society now where many mothers choose not to breastfeed because they don't want to "spoil" their figures. But this is at the cost of missing out on that special bonding.

Titus 2:3–5 says, "The older women likewise, that they be reverent in behavior, not slanderers, not given to much wine, teachers of good things—that they admonish the young women to love their husbands, to love their children, to be discreet, chaste, homemakers, good, obedient to their own husbands, that the word of God may not be blasphemed."

Every mother should use this scripture as an example to teach the young ones Godly character, domestic responsibility, and integrity, that motherhood be celebrated. They must teach their children how to dress and, in particular, teach the girls how to dress modestly.

We are now seeing that men are dressing like prisoners with their pants waist almost below the knee and women wearing their underwear in public and that this has become the norm! The standards have not fallen; they have plummeted, and mothers must raise the standard—they have the capacity to do it!

Mothers for Change

The mother is the first one to teach their children to honor God with their finances (Proverbs 3:9–10). A good mother teaches her children about the principles and the goodness of God and how to pray and to honor their (earthly) fathers—even if they are not good fathers. What has seriously affected the society is the fact that many women have taught the younger generation to hate the fathers that have neglected them. Instead, they should teach them to forgive those fathers who have reneged their responsibilities toward them.

Don't teach them to curse the irresponsible fathers, and don't call them worthless sperm donors. Teach them that despite all that, they can change the game and do better.

Many curse the men for not supporting their children but refuse to acknowledge the role of some women who hinder their men from taking care of the children external to their relationship.

Motherhood/Leadership

The mother is the one who teaches her sons that when they are placed in positions of leadership, they must not womanize, be drunkards, show injustice, and oppress the poor and needy (Proverbs 31:2–9) but, instead, speak up on behalf of the poor and honor the women in their lives.

They must teach their children that once in authority, they must measure to higher standards than the mere average.

Inherent in every good mother is a wife, a visionary, and a businesswoman who has several business ventures that will help her family. She enjoys the confidence of all her family. She is a watchman over the family and helps to deal with the emotional and spiritual condition of her family. She is a prayer warrior who births the vision of her husband and children, encouraging them to pursue their dream. She engages in real estate transactions, using the profits for further investment as a security for her family. She will never be afraid to tell her children the truth when they are wrong; neither does she teach any form of rebellion or division within the family. She unites her family and prays for her church, her country, and her place of work.

MEN AND WOMEN

CHAPTER 12

WHAT MEN WANT, WHAT WOMEN WANT

Now more than ever, we need to get back to the basics. Marriages are under attack! God's intention was for man to experience the oneness of authentic love and true, genuine relationship. Sexual relationship was meant to be enjoyed by married couples. God created sexual intimacy for the purpose of procreation and a physical symbol of unity. It is to be enjoyed regularly by married couple and to avoid the temptation of doing something God did not ordain. It must be maintained in wholesomeness, faithfulness, purity of heart, discipline of eye, and consecration of the body (Matthew 5:27–28; Job 31:1).

Men and women were created from two different processes! Man was formed; woman was made. For both to understand each other, it takes a process. God will fashion the man first so that he becomes more sensitive to the woman (Jeremiah 18).

Nothing can be made without it first being formed (Genesis 2). The first recorded administration of anesthetics, and the first operation and the first transplant took place in Genesis 2:21, where the man's right rib was taken out to make the right fit for him. Thus, a man must ensure that the woman who is to be his wife is the right fit. That being said, here are the questions: What do men want? What do women want?

What Men Want

Men want peace in their relationships; no nagging. They love good food, and a lot of it, presented well. They also want a good facial from their wives from time to time and a weekly massage. (This will help keep them away from a third party.) They need women that encourage them and defend their vision and encourage them to work; and when others want to tear them down, they want a woman who will stand up for and with them and defend them—be in their corner. They want a woman who spends their money wisely and is a problem solver—that can take a little, especially in this bad economy, and turn it around. They want a woman who is a good communicator and negotiator who will represent them well. These women must be women of prayer and must in no way compete with their husbands but work with him in their different areas and work toward one goal for the family. Men like to run their hands through a woman's hair. They want a woman who is well groomed, and they want a woman who will be a good mother to their children and set the right examples for them. They like a woman who is classy, not boisterous. Men like to be complimented on occasion by their wives—letting them know how good they look or how well they might have done something. Men like to be cuddled, too, and they love a good head rub! (Songs of Solomon 2:6). The next thing that the men love is found in Songs of Solomon 1:13!

What Women Want

Women want to know that their men care about them beyond sex! They want a genuine relationship that allows them to know that they have security and commitment from their husbands. Women do not want to be compared with other women. Women want their ideas/dreams supported—especially by their husbands. Women want to know that even as they go out to play their role outside the home, their husbands are willing to help within the home setting—share the load. Women want to know that their husbands will help with the children too. Women love to spend time together with each other and have a good time. Women want to have a good time and enjoy banquets and socials. Women want to be fed and treated well by their husbands—fed with apples and raisins and cakes and pleasant things. Women love to smell good they love fragrances and nice clothes. Women love to communicate! They have a lot to say, and they like it when their husbands listen. For a woman, it is *how* you say what you say to her that counts. Some may feel rejected when at a certain age they don't have children. Never tell a woman she is barren! Many good women take a while to conceive—the Hannahs, the Rebeccas, and the Sarahs! Never forget birthdays, anniversaries, or other special occasions—you will not live it down! So ensure that you stockpile a lot of gifts! Remember this: a woman is not finished after she has children; she is just beginning to walk into another dimension of who she is. Never let her feel rejected after children; that is the time to celebrate her. Women like to be celebrated.

Finally, when problems arise, always remember that man was formed, women were made. Men and women are built differently, with different roles, so different approaches are needed—but for one goal!

It is time for us to rebuild the family!

Things That Matter . . .

To a Woman

A real woman doesn't need money or a multitude of things to make her happy in a relationship. What she truly needs is the support and admiration of the man in her life. There needs to be more training in the church for the men to learn how to treat a woman. This is what many women have said. For a real woman, her family is what truly matters to her, and if the man in her life is not in his proper position, then there will be problems in the relationship. The man is the head and the leader of the family, and if the head is not connected to the body, then the body cannot function effectively if at all.

Many women I have interviewed have said that they want a man who is spiritually mature—one who is willing to take the time to understand them and one who will pray for them. A real woman wants a man, not a boy—and certainly not a mama's boy! A real woman wants a man who will speak positive words over her and encourage her—a man who is sober in the faith and who walks in the Fruit of the Spirit (Galatians 5).

Titus 2:2 looks at these very same characteristics for a man that women want to see in men today—"that the older men be sober, reverent, temperate, sound in faith, in love, in patience . . ." These characteristics not only strengthen the relationship but also lead to a sound church, and we are the church.

Women need the men they love to support their dreams and visions. A woman wants the man she loves to be there for her in times of weakness, and to be understanding. She wants to feel valued by the one they love. Women like to be shown affection and to be given flowers, surprises, and other gifts; but they *do not* like to be compared with other women. Women need to have financial security and financial peace not just for herself but for her family.

Women need men with solid foundation built from a strong Spiritual background. They need someone who understands the difference in them and is not afraid to invest in them and is not intimidated by their success. A man with a strong Spiritual foundation will not be afraid to pray for the prosperity for his woman; nor is he afraid to give strong moral, physical, or financial support to his queen. She will not be afraid to cry on the shoulders of her husband.

A true woman's number-one desire is not materialistic. She is more interested in fulfilling her God-given purpose. Through my counseling sessions, I have realized that it is very difficult to find men with such qualities as were outlined before. Sadly, many of them are rotting away in prisons or gangs, or are on drugs, because of the failure of the fathers who are absent from mentoring their sons on how to walk into greatness.

Women see the characteristics of a good man as one who

- puts the welfare of his family first;
- depends on God to lead and direct him;
- acknowledges God as his Head;

- pulls his strength from God;
- is unafraid to honor God in public;
- shows honor to parents and leaders at all levels;
- stands up for truth;
- walks in integrity, holiness, and sexual purity; and
- shows respect to her and to his family.

To a Man

Having interviewed quite a number of men, especially through counseling sessions, the number-one issue that came up was the frustration of not being able to "release" when there is "build up"—sex. A man, having been created different from a woman, needs the immediate access to enjoy intimacy with the woman he loves.

But when asked to prioritize, this is what men say matters to them:

- sex
- food
- don't embarrass them before friends
- woman who is trustworthy
- want women to support their vision
- helpmeet
- likes to be pampered and be made to feel like a king
- to be encouraged by the woman he loves
- want to know that she will make time for him
- like to show off their wives—they are proud of who is by his side
- want a woman who knows the Word of God and will pray
- relationship with God

Real men are looking for inner beauty, not external beauty. Inner beauty deals with a person's attitude, personality, and character. In spiritual terms, we call it the Fruit of the Spirit or a Virtuous Woman (Proverbs 31). They are looking for someone who will stand with them in good times and bad. They are not looking for a woman who is rebellious or one who engages in feminism, is greedy for money, or is self-absorbed.

They are looking for someone who will put the family first and who is not easily influenced by the world's ways.

This is why most famous or influential men always go looking for simple persons to marry who are not frightened or influenced by fame or beauty but are more interested in inward beauty.

External beauty will not keep a man as some women may think. The man wants to know that the woman has his back—that her motives are pure, that she is not driven by every wind of doctrine and not driven by material things, competing with other women on who has the latest. A real man is looking for loyalty and someone he is not afraid to allow him to have access to their financial transactions. He wants someone who will not waste their resources on the wrong things, but helps him to build an empire and inheritance for their children. He is not looking for someone who will run to the media at the drop of a hat if something should go wrong. Furthermore, men don't need women who will expose themselves in public—where the most private and precious parts of her are open to public viewing. Real men understand that what is most precious is always hidden waiting to be found, not put in a place of commonness, and recognize that the joy is in the finding. Gold and diamonds are always hidden and are worth finding. Real men know that once his wife has good qualities, she will teach their daughter(s).

Every woman needs to know that she is valuable. Real men recognize that women who expose themselves are simply reducing their value. Men will want to sleep with them but will not want to marry them. Real men recognize that any adult female is a woman, but a lady is a woman who carries herself with a certain level of grace and class.

Real men need women who have a gentle and quiet spirit whose focus is on the internal and not just the external. They want women who fear God.

Real men know that when God brings a woman through testing, it is to create greater inner beauty so that when elevation takes place, lawyers will not become the beneficiaries and recipients of the fruit of their labor.

Real men understand that the results of inner beauty are as stated in Proverbs 3:16–18, that "She is more precious than rubies, and all the things you may desire cannot compare with her. Length of days is in her right hand, in her left hand riches and honor. Her ways are ways of pleasantness, and all her paths are peace. She is a tree of life to those who take hold of her, and happy are all who retain her."

Adornment starts from the inside (1 Peter 3:3). The world's way of adorning is external, while they ignore the internal adorning God wants done. Too much emphasis is placed on clothing, cosmetics, and other external matters, while the internal beautification is being ignored. That is why many times, Christian women will complain about their husband's not coming to church without realizing that their actions and attitudes are turning them away from coming to the Lord (1 Peter 3:1–6).

Men and Women of Purpose Arise!

Have you ever felt incomplete? Have you ever felt unhappy regardless of what you have accomplished? Have you been feeling restless recently and are getting dreams and visions, some of which you don't understand? Some of you are just going to work for a salary/pay, but there is no joy in what you are doing. Some of you just watch the clock. Some of you have had near-death experiences and suffer many things—disappointment, extreme adversities, abuse, and even things you don't tell anyone, but by yourselves you cry. Many of you have tried to fit in with the boys or girls, but it doesn't work. You are different!

When God creates you with greatness inside you, then you have to be set apart—you are an eagle, and an eagle does not sit with chickens. That is why you feel odd and incomplete. Even when you have retired and there is still a fire burning within you, then it means that there is still more within you and you have not yet fulfilled your purpose!

Each person was created to solve a problem. Many times when we see chaos, economic problems, injustice, crises with our children—those things come about because the one who was created to deal with that problem is not in proper position. Each time we pray or cry out to God to bring change to an organization or a nation, the answer always lies within a human vessel. That is why Jesus Christ always focused on building the vessel first. God created the earth and equipped it with all He created in it before, and then He placed mankind in it. Likewise, He created us—the human vessels—and has equipped us with the solutions within us for the problems that we would encounter.

Within each person is embedded instructions to carry out, and when they fail to carry out their assignment, many lives and many things are at stake. Your education is not your purpose, and for many, your job is not your purpose. Some of the clues to your purpose include the things that make you angry when they happen but bring you great joy when they are addressed or fixed—the things that grieve you.

When you see disorder in the society, how do you feel about it? Do you become extremely angry? It indicates that you are a born leader. Leadership is a gift given by God (Romans 8:7; Romans 12:7–8). Likewise, teaching is a God-given gift! Now we see why there are so many problems within the education system. Some of the wrong people are in the classrooms.

You Don't Decide Your Purpose

God is the One Who decides your purpose! He is the One Who places you in the geographical location He wants you to be to fulfill your assignment. When you resist your purpose, painful things occur in your life. That is why we ought to be against abortion, because our purpose is decided before we are conceived. Jeremiah 1 specifically states it. Whether we believe in the existence of God or not does not change that.

There are some people within the nation, whether we like them or not, and regardless of our political affiliation, who have greatness within them, and if they fulfill their purpose, great change can come.

- Barry "Barry G" Gordon (Jamaica) has the ability to bring revival within the nation among the youth. He is a prophet from his mother's womb.
- SSP James Forbes (Jamaica) has a Pastoral calling. He can bring change to the inner city and within the police force. He should read Matthew 6 and John 3. God must be his only source. If he should fulfill his purpose, great turnaround will take place.

- Gordon "Butch" Stewart (Jamaica) has the solution for a business revolution. If he should focus on fulfilling his purpose, things would unveil within him that he never knew was there.
- The Honorable Bruce O. Golding (Jamaica)—his work is not over yet. There are solutions within him to bring change politically and economically.
- Paula Llewellyn, CD QC (Jamaica), Director of Public Prosecution (DPP), has gifts in her to mentor, motivate, teach, and counsel. She can do great things to help the abused girls.
- Fae Ellington, OD (Jamaica), has a gift to bring back order particularly to the state of women within the nation.
- Beverley Anderson-Duncan (Jamaica) has great revelation within her to bring change within the nation.
- The Honorable K. D. Knight (Jamaica) has a gift to establish proper governance and human rights.
- The Honorable Peter Phillips (Jamaica) has the gift of administration and Pastoral calling.
- Justice Martin Gayle (Jamaica) has within the capacity to reform the justice system as well as to mentor young lawyers and judges.
- Rexton "Shabba Ranks" Gordon (Jamaica) has a gift for community transformation.
- Police Commissioner Owen Ellington (Jamaica)—his gifts address politics, youth, and community. He would be a good Youth Minister.
- Marcia Griffiths (Jamaica) has a gift to mentor and counsel, and she has the gift of compassion.
- President Barack Obama (USA)—God wants him to lecture in the universities, be a humanitarian outreach person, and also to work in the inner city communities.
- The Honorable Portia Simpson-Miller (Jamaica)—God wants her to raise up her own university.
- The Lord wants to use Shaquille O'Neal (USA)—he has an Apostolic calling on his life to transform communities, working with troubled teens/youth and setting up foundations for scholarships.
- Duane Wade (USA) has a (youth) Pastoral calling.

- Mariah Carey's (USA) calling is a Prophetess.
- Hillary Clinton (USA) has a mighty teaching ministry and an evangelical ministry.
- Denzel Washington (USA) has quite the Pastoral calling on his life and a gift to motivate the youth.

Imagine if each person begins to fulfill his/her purpose, what major changes would take place.

CHAPTER 13

PARENTS: THE FIRST
ROLE MODELS

We are living in a time where immorality is getting more coverage and attention than crime, poverty, and social injustice, and we are now seeing men apologizing for speaking and standing up for fundamental truth. One of the greatest requirements on the Church is the capacity to discern between the spiritual struggle and other social, personal, and political difficulties. Otherwise, individual parents must understand and must recognize that they are wrestling not with human adversaries but against the invisible forces working against families.

Since the family is the key component within society, proper relationships must be maintained. All must know that the family is the first governing institution from Creation.

Recognize that poor family upbringing yields poor leadership and, thus, a poor society. If the family is what makes the society, then we need to have a separate ministry that will be responsible for the family. Part of the qualifications for those who will *lead* that ministry is that they must be experienced couples.

Shapers and Motivators

Parents are the first role models for their children, and their responsibilities include motivating and shaping the minds of their children in such a way that they are not easily swayed by negative influencers but that, instead, they will make good choices to foster a healthy society. It is the parents' responsibility to teach their children about abstinence, premarital sex, and extramarital sex. They must know the spiritual and physical dangers of these activities. Parents need to teach them the importance and significance of acquiring sound education. They must teach their children that their bodies are of great value and that it is in fact God's temple—not just *a* temple!

Parents must recognize that simply issuing or supporting the issue of condoms throughout schools and even at home is promoting early and premarital sexual activity—not to mention promiscuity—all in the name of boosting revenue from condom sales.

It is the responsibility of parents to teach their children the benefits of the children honoring their parents (Exodus 20:12). God promised extended life to parents who would grow their children in the fear of God (Deuteronomy 7:3–4). Teach them when they awaken each morning, before they go to bed, when you sit together at the dinner table (which needs to come back), and when they walk with you on the streets!

Parents must

- guide their children from an early age concerning whom they marry—wrong choices bring problems!
- teach their children to obey rules and the laws of the land;
- teach their children to stay away from drugs, illicit activities, the wrong doctrine, and even the wrong attitudes toward others. They must let them know that there are people within the society who will influence them to carry and engage in all kinds of things and that they must stay away from them.
- recognize that there are people and organizations that benefit when their children go down the wrong path (jail, funeral homes);
- understand that the same persons that influence their children to do the wrong things are the same ones who influence the

authorities to get rid of their children—whether to shoot them or imprison them!

- pray for (not against) the children of others because you never know if in doing so you are protecting your own children;

- spend the time to watch the shows and scrutinize the video games that their children have. Look for the subtle messages that sensitize and pull them to the wrong things and stir up wrong attitudes in them.

- recognize that the popularity and level of intelligence of an individual is not what makes them a good role model. There are many influential and popular people in the society, but if night should turn into day, there would be shocking revelations!

- do spot checks on what is being taught to or done with their children at school. Oftentimes, they allow the children to watch movies parents wouldn't or don't want them to watch. Sometimes gifts are given as prizes that parents may not want their child/ children to receive. Sometimes the curriculum includes things that you would not want taught to your child/children yet or at all.

Additionally, a father must recognize that he is the first man in his daughter's life; a mother must recognize that she is the first woman in her son's life and that each parent, therefore, sets the standard for them to follow when choosing a spouse.

Parenting

Psalm 127:3 says, "Behold, children are a heritage from the Lord, the fruit of the womb is a reward."

We are living in a time where modern technology is the order of the day, and parents should in no way be naïve about what is taking place in our world. There are many things designed to destroy our children, all in the name of greed and moneymaking. There are many who pledge allegiance to their God for prosperity and power, and they will do anything to make money, including destroying your children.

Parents, you are the police of your household, and you must begin to properly police what enters and exits your household—whether technological or physical. It is the responsibility of every parent to supervise their children—what they eat, wear, listen to, read, watch, and play, and their manners. Many parents today are allowing the children to be the parents, and God will hold the parents responsible. The children are not your friends—they are your responsibilities. They are a heritage. They are given to us to train and mold. As parents, you must scrutinize the very friends they keep and the backgrounds from which those friends come. The enemy will use negative/bad influences to indoctrinate them. The enemy wants to destroy the children. It is why we are seeing terrorists and human traffickers groom them from an early age. Some are even groomed to be part of the occult. Different organizations who are funded by the occult and others with purely evil intentions are issuing tablets and other technological devices to entice our children and youth under the guise of helping them to become more technologically advanced, aware, and equipped. Meanwhile, those behind it are kidnapping them with the intention of selling them to unscrupulous persons or groups.

The movie industry in the West has been carefully indoctrinating our children subtly as part of their strategic plan. They know that the eyes are one of the gates to our souls. What we hear and see can defile our souls and then manifest physically—so much so that even as they go to bed, they are getting dreams that are not of God. Parents today—*you* cannot afford to be naïve.

I have seen parents buy expensive electronic gifts, and after watching it, children become possessed with demonic influences, and it affects their grades. Advanced technology must be used to do good things and solve problems.

Much of the crime taking place globally with the children is a result of the things to which they are exposed—including the games they are playing (Luke 11:34–35; Matthew 18:19). Some of our churches are deceived as they celebrate Halloween and invite magicians into the House of God and refuse to teach the children about the root of Halloween and magic.

The foundation of good parenting is teaching our children the truth. Each time we pray to God to bless us, He gives us Spiritual and/

or biological children. Never compromise with their upbringing. Always remember that society will always behave as if they care, but society today has built more prisons than educational facilities in this era.

God has outlined in His Word that there are benefits to good parenting, including long life to us as parents,

The Best Parenting Handbook

The family is the first line of government, and with the failing of the family structure globally, parents need and must necessarily use the best parenting handbook—the Bible—as a guide to good parenting.

1) Teach your children to be in obedience to both spiritual and biological parents, especially those parents who are Christians. Obedience determines their success and longevity of their lives (Ephesians 6:1–3).

2) When children fail to honor earthly parents, they will not learn to honor God either. This will bring instability in the family and affect the social fabric of the nation (Deuteronomy 5:16).

3) When parents fail to teach their children, the entire nation suffers, and that is what is now causing the spiritual drought now affecting nations (Exodus 20:12).

4) Teach your children about sound financial responsibility by teaching them about Tithing and the giving of Offerings.

5) Maintain good communication with your children using God's Word as the number-one criterion when training them. Avoid any destructive doctrine or philosophy. Communicate with them at the dinner table, when you're walking or driving, when you are going to bed at night, or rising up in the morning! (Deuteronomy 6:6–9).

6) Teach your children the goodness of God daily, as well as the power of prayer! Share your testimony with them.

7) Teach your children how to choose with regard to relationships of all kinds—personal and business. Let them know they are to avoid becoming unequally yoked and to avoid relationships

with people who refuse to serve the same God as they serve. Let them know that the vision of those they want to connect with in relationships must be in line with their vision (Deuteronomy 23:8–12).

8) Good choices are key to success! The choices determine the inheritance of your children.

9) Teach your children to avoid tattoos and sex before marriage. Let them know that their virginity is priceless! Keep them away from perverted music and movies.

10) Teach your children how to obey God's voice daily (Deuteronomy 28:1–14).

11) Pray a hedge of protection around your children—as Job did! (Job 1:1–4).

12) Teach your children about the different roles that each parent plays. For example, the mother nurtures the children and the father instills discipline (Proverbs 1:8–9).

13) The father should use the Word of God and allow the Holy Spirit to help him to carry out discipline and his fatherly role.

14) Declare blessings over your children daily (Colossians 3:21; Ephesians 6:4; Proverbs 29:15; Proverbs 13:24; Proverbs 19:18; Proverbs 22:15).

15) When parents fail to discipline their children, we fail and we hate our children. Failure will bring shame and disgrace on the family.

CHAPTER 14

GOD CARES FOR THE SINGLE PARENTS

It is very difficult for single parents to survive in a society where there are serious social, moral, and economic problems. Single parents have been going through a great deal—some are jobless, and they are the main income earner for their families, not only for their children but also for their siblings. This is even more so for those who are attending school in an effort to achieve more in life. As a result of such challenges, there are numerous temptations that exist—including prostitution, drug peddling, and even running away from their families and responsibilities. There needs to be a greater collaborative work among the Churches, NGOs (Non-Governmental Organizations), businesses, and the government to set up programs that can be beneficial to all, especially to single parents.

Let us first recognize that the term "single parent" does not in totality refer to a promiscuous unmarried female who gets pregnant and has a child. There are widows and widowers with children, divorcees with sole custody, and aunts or uncles who must parent the children of a sibling.

There are numerous situations that result in someone becoming a single parent.

A simple discount or even a part-time job to assist them can go a far way. Even cutting back on some of the cash programs and redirecting it to education for them can bring significant and positive results.

Many of them are being abused for survival's sake, but there are several scriptures where God provides for single parents including Exodus 22:22–25, 1 Kings 17:8–16, and 2 Kings 4. Furthermore, Isaiah 54:5 gives a powerful reassurance.

God intervenes in their lives and provides spiritually and physically and even rescues them from the onslaught of financial institutions.

There are many families in society who have lost a spouse who serves in the military or police force and have received no help—financially or otherwise. Some are cheated out of their inheritance through the use of clauses.

The Source of Help

Single parents, look first to God as your Source! Many are looking for a man/woman as their source for survival. Always remember that God will restore those who faithfully wait on Him to be married or remarried. Tenacity is the key. Waiting is essential for one's development—because among other things, waiting reveals the heart, strengthens us, and protects us.

Many single parents, because they want the physical help or they want to satisfy certain physical desires (usually sex), turn to what they are accustomed, what they used to do—they run back even to past abusive relationships. Some are told that nobody wants them because they already have children. Walk out of the rejection, shake off negative words, and embrace and pursue your purpose! You are in process for a greater purpose.

Even single women at times have been rejected by men who say they refuse to marry anyone who was already married or who already has children. Such persons need to renew their minds and embrace the Divine will if they want to be successful.

Never be quick to jump out of the process of your single life, because there is a purpose for which you are being molded. You will need all the training and experience for the task ahead. Seek experienced and righteous mentors who will help to mold and develop you. Servanthood, submission, loyalty, steadfastness, and tenacity to purpose will become of the keys to moving forward.

Women need to know that good men are looking at the heart condition—attitude and character.

Men need to know that good women are looking for men of integrity with backbone who will love and take care of his wife and family. They want to know that they will embrace the children she already has, as his, too—to love and treat them as if they were his own.

Single people, continue to "glean in the field" that God has provided for you. Stop walking from church to church in an effort to shorten your process. Ensure that whomever you are serving—whether your Pastor or your secular boss—you serve faithfully and respectfully, because it all adds up.

Words of Wisdom

Remember, persistence is the key to your breakthrough. If you dedicate one hour of your social networking time to prayer, your dream might just become reality more quickly than you expect. Every good man desires a praying woman—even an atheist. God honors a servantleader, so serve and volunteer with all your heart.

Maintain your purity. Each time you mess up, the process may become longer. And when you are "on fire," ask the Lord to cool the fire until He brings the right "fire stick" to rekindle the fire!

Make vows and sacrifices. I have seen people abstain from certain foods or activities to receive the promise of God and are today enjoying their breakthrough and the desires of their hearts!

God honors sacrifice!

Enjoy Your Single Life

I believe being married is the number-one thing on the list of every single woman. Many want to get married even more than getting an education. Some believe that there is a shortage of men, particularly in the church.

Many single women make compromises, which lead to hurt, joining themselves in unholy yokes and wrong relationships. However, let me encourage you; don't be in a rush to get married.

People will often complain that they do not want to remain single because of their age, and they want to fulfill sexual desires. However, getting married means more than that. Marriage is a lifetime covenant, and God uses the time that you are single to process you. He wants to correct the flaws, attitudes, or mind-set that you might have about relationships and marriage. Furthermore, God wants to bring healing to you from past hurts and broken relationships.

Some people say, as the saying goes, "Marriage is a bed of roses." They are absolutely right, because there are a lot of "thorns" that can prick you. The Mills & Boon perspective is a fantasy—that the perfectly chiseled man and the woman with the perfect body marry and live happily ever after. However, marriage is about suppressing your desires and embracing the "us," "our," and "we" in the relationship.

Many women who are entrepreneurs or other business professionals don't believe that man is the head of the family, so submission can be a factor that can terminate marriage quickly.

Many women don't know what they want or whom they are looking for. When asked, many suggest the following: lots of money, good sex, a strong man, an intellectual, someone like daddy, childless, white or brown—no black, no police, soldier, or uniformed men, and no Pastor.

In God's view, none of the above matters when preparing you for marriage. What is important is your purpose and your choice—whether the person lines up with God's vision and purpose for your life. You could marry a man who kills your vision and purpose. You have to ensure that God fits you with the right rib. In a sense, it is like how the parts of a Lexus and Benz don't work together.

CHAPTER 15

ABOUT DATING AND MARRIAGE

D ating or courting is such a sensitive issue for many Christians, and even for the Church. There are a number of single people (whether they have never been married before or are divorced) who are seeking for a life partner and are hoping to identify one by going out with them on a regular basis without any kind of real commitment. There are others who don't want a life partner but prefer to satisfy desires as they arise without any kind of long-term commitment. Then there are those who are afraid of disappointment and hurt and prefer not to commit. So dating becomes their "solution" of choice.

Whatever the basis for dating, it does not reveal true motives or willingness to commit. Dating simply gives many an excuse to enjoy the benefits of a long-term committed relationship that should be sealed with the bond of marriage—*without* the commitment. This leads to actions and activities opposite to God's instructions and will for us and causes the development of unholy soul ties. It clouds an individual's judgment and skews his/her mind-set.

Biblically, there must be a "leaving and cleaving" that ought to take place (Mark 10:7–9; Genesis 2:24). It is in the process of cleaving (spiritual bonding) that the character flaws and physical capabilities many want to identify beforehand become clearer.

Marriage is a spiritual issue, because the cleaving that takes place is not physical; it is a spiritual experience. Dating is a physical action that is based on what is literally seen. So our commitment has to be based on more than the physical and begs the question therefore, "Who does God have for us?"

Steps to Follow

Biblically speaking, it is not the woman who should be seeking (or hunting) the man. The man must seek and find his wife. (If the man has to date in order to know whether or not this union would be what God wants, then he has missed the boat somewhere.) His goal should be to seek the Lord for the answer.

Proverbs 18:22 reminds us: "He who finds a wife finds a good thing, and obtains favor from the LORD." *Putting a ring on it* is not what makes a woman a wife, and it is not about practicing regular sexual encounters or your capacity to "keep house"! It is her grace under pressure, her capacity to go through hardship and difficult times without "jumping ship" or bailing out. It is her strength of character, integrity, and capacity to keep a unit of differing personalities together under all circumstances; it is the qualities she possesses and her spiritual, mental, and emotional maturity that prepare her for that long-term role.

Men, love your wife as Christ loves the Church. Love means that you must be willing to lay your life down (literally and otherwise) for your wife and family. It means you must stand by your wife and family no matter what and not run away and leave them to fend for themselves. It means you must lead from the front, provide for your family in every way possible, and stand strong in difficult times.

Yes, marriage *is* a bed of roses, but remember roses also have thorns, so we must expect to get pricked from time to time and still hold it together and not complain.

Many today use social networks to advertise themselves and their "availability." This is not what God would want for you. You are not a piece of merchandise for bidding; you are of greater value than that to God.

Entering into marriage covenants that cause you to become "unequally yoked" is not what God would want for you (2 Corinthians 6:15).

Once the man identifies that this is the woman who will be his wife, he then needs to go to her family—especially to her father, and let him know his intentions toward the lady. Once the family/father agrees, then they ought to approach their spiritual leader who would carry them through premarital counseling. There should be an announcement and then the engagement/betrothal. After that, a date for the wedding should be set, and it should not be indefinite! While no one can dictate a specific date to those involved, why wait for years if the person you have identified is the one that God has sanctioned? If money is a problem, then this is where the families on both sides have the opportunity to come together, support the couple, and help them to get a good start off.

Christians, remember 2 Peter 2:9.

Premarital Relations and Marriage

As a Christian, don't approach someone for a serious relationship unless you are willing and ready to be married. Many times people get engaged and believe that it is a free pass to have sex with the person to whom they are engaged.

Engagement is not a trial period. In the Bible, there was a betrothal. A betrothal was like a private ceremony before the outward celebration and was a major and binding commitment (Deuteronomy 20:5–7; Deuteronomy 24:5). This was especially so for those who went to war.

A *betrothal* was the period of engagement preceding marriage and was a binding contract established between two families and sealed by the exchange of gifts. During this period, the couple did not live together, and sexual relations with each other at this stage were regarded as equivalent to adultery. Betrothal describes the relationship between God and his people and between Jesus Christ and the Church.

Today, people live together and have sex with each other, and after several months or years after or after becoming pregnant or after having children, they present themselves to get married. Many say they are engaged and then engage themselves in sex. Then after a while, the engagement is off, and there was no real commitment; they move on to someone else.

When a couple sits before or presents themselves to a marriage counselor or Pastor for premarital counseling, they must have already made up their minds that no matter what, this is my husband/wife. It is not a trial period; it is a serious thing. Furthermore, the couple must meet the criterion of not being equally yoked.

It is the man who is supposed to seek the Lord for guidance on who is supposed to be his wife. After God has revealed that, he is to approach both sets of parents for their blessings. Both persons must meet the standard of being equally yoked. An ox and a donkey can't pull the plow together. Once all the requirements are met and the approvals have been given, then they go directly into premarital counseling where a wedding date will be set for marriage. The wedding date should not be a long wait from the time it was set to the time it is executed. Boundaries need to be set during the waiting period so that fornication does not take place. It is critical, when one is getting married, to start with a good foundation so that "soul tie" issues don't take place. Seventy percent of the people I counsel oftentimes fornicate before the marriage takes place. As a result, they give the enemy legal right to invoke curses. Many after marriage, because of fornication before the marriage, have a number of spiritual, sexual, and financial problems that come about because of the door opened as a result of their premarital actions. There are always consequences for sin. It is critical for single people to ensure that that they create good covenants and have good footing when they are established in a marriage covenant. Sinning against your body carries serious consequences. The body is the temple of the Lord.

There are many people who break up quickly after marriage because they fornicated. Some even want to blame their pastors for their choices and the consequences. Un-Godly covenants established through sex, diseases, and other issues will take place. Sexual sin has become one of the top issues globally. The enemy is using it as a stronghold to keep people in bondage. There are many who need deliverance from this matter because of sexual impurity. Christians are now struggling because they are unable to remain pure.

Single

God loves and cares for single people. It is critical for single people to keep serving until the one God chooses for them comes. God is able to make up for lost time—age doesn't matter. God knows the right fit. It is not easy to be single, because the enemy often brings great temptation by stirring up sexual urges and impatience—which is a dangerous combination. Furthermore, if you surround yourself with poor/bad influences, you run the high risk of falling into temptation.

Surround yourself with strong support. Avoid certain situations such as going to the beach with members of the opposite sex, going clubbing, watching certain movies, or engaging in masturbation and using sex toys.

God has a waiting process through which He brings single people through to consecrate them. He wants to work on your inward beauty. A woman must be a wife before she is married. Marriage doesn't make a woman a wife; it simply makes it official.

Recognize that disobedience can delay the process of marriage. Ensure that you are obedient to the instructions and the Word of God.

Know that

- your main focus must be on God;
- you must be in the Word of God;
- you must maintain a strong prayer life; and
- you must continue to develop your educational background while waiting.

Do not be afraid to talk to your leaders about your struggles so they can encourage you. Speak to married leaders.

Prayer for Single People

Father, in the name of Jesus,
Help me, Lord, to be strong.
Keep my mind pure and focused on You.
Help me not to fall into temptation.
Pour out Your grace on my life to endure temptation.
Keep me from every trap set for me to fall into fornication.
Sharpen my discerning to know Your will and Your
    purpose for me.
Fix me, Lord, while I wait so that I may not resist Your will.
Let every desire of my choice die to Your choice while I wait.
I thank you Lord for Your coverage, protection, and provision while I
    wait.
In Jesus' name. Amen.

Choosing a Wife

Choosing a wife is one of the most important things a man can do. It determines the success or failure in a man's life and work. Regardless of the vision or a person's purpose, marrying the wrong person can destroy one's purpose or destiny.

Abraham knew the importance of marrying the right person, especially regarding wealth transfer. He wanted to ensure that with his hard work, the wealth that will be transferred remains in the family. Choosing a wife has to do with genealogy and is very important, because of the lineage you will become a part of determines a lot. In the Bible, lineage and genealogy are very important, particularly regarding blessings and curses.

The next thing in choosing a wife is to ensure that your choice is accepted by your parent(s), especially your father. They have the authority to agree or disagree with your choice.

Most men, when choosing a wife, are totally ignorant of the criteria they should look for to have a successful marriage. Most are looking for outward attractiveness, academic qualifications, and money, and oftentimes the physical appearance they are pursuing lands them into trouble. All these criteria just mentioned are not Biblical, and when looking for a wife, the man has to allow God to choose that wife for him. They have to have the same passions, goals/objectives, and faith. He must remember that she is a part of him, so anything that is not in God's will means there will be unequal yoking, and being unequally yoked will bring disaster.

In Genesis 2:18, it speaks about a "helper," which indicates that Adam's strength for all he was called to be and do was inadequate in itself. Comparable to him denotes complementarity. The need for "helper" is for daily work, procreation, and mutual support through companionship. Hence, having God's choice and the right pick is very critical. With all the responsibilities God gave Adam, which include naming things, God had to put him to sleep and performed the first surgery so that Adam would have the right choice. Man has to seek God and allow Him to choose for him; then the woman would become the right fit—bone of his bone and flesh of his flesh. This is what you call creative miracles. Choosing the right wife gives you favor with God and man, protects your inheritance, and prevents unnecessary legal costs in the future, and you would also get someone with a servant's heart, as we see in Genesis 24. Abraham's servant chose a wife for his master's son. She carried over four hundred gallons of water for the camels of a stranger.

Every husband needs a wife who is a hard worker—one with great mercy and compassion, someone willing to go the extra mile, someone who is willing to walk away from her town, her family, and one who will not go without the blessing of their parents (Genesis 24:60–63) and who recognizes that the blessing of her parents is important.

Prayer brings God's will into our lives. It brings confirmation, parental blessings, wisdom, and Godly mate/choice. Many ignore the application of prayer and Biblical Principles and then become bitter and blame God. Please take note that it was not the wife who goes to search for a husband but the man who goes to find his wife. It is not about a trial to see if it would work. You would wake up and be hit by reality. Good sex before marriage is not a criterion. Some may say that they will not get married before they "sample the product," but don't be fooled by that.

This will only result in un-Godly soul ties. Love is a learning process. It takes time to grow.

Making decisions based on sex means that you're making a decision with your reproductive organ and not your brain. God and love will sustain you. Likewise, the wedding day is not what decides that she is wife. Proverbs 18:22 states, "He that finds a wife, finds a good thing and obtains favor from the Lord." It did not say he that finds a woman. It is not God's will for man to be alone. They must to come together to help each other to fulfill their individual and collective purposes.

CHAPTER 16

OUR CHILDREN—OUR HERITAGE!

With the worldwide crises now affecting the children, many are giving different opinions on what is to be done; some blame parenting skills. What we are realizing is that a parent cannot impart what they themselves have never experienced. We now have to rebuild the foundation and build it on and with truth.

There are many "truths" in this world today, but there is only one right Truth (Proverbs 16:25; Proverbs 14:12). It is all our duty to win our youth over from philosophical views. They must be made to understand that man's views, wisdom or reasoning is NOT superior to God's! (Colossians 2:8) We need to teach our youth how to deal with/handle subtle reasoning (Colossians 2:4) that would steer them away from the truth.

There are many "lights" in this world, and the enemy seeks out brilliant, intellectual, powerful, and popular people that he can influence and use, to reach others to influence their way of thinking. The failure of the church leaders over the years is that they were diluting the truth to facilitate this generation because they did not know how to deal with them; neither did they have a new revelation of the Word itself. They have abandoned the "Old Gate" (Nehemiah 3) and have allowed New

Age philosophies to infiltrate our youth. We are bringing in these new philosophies and Hollywood syndrome to suit the desires of man. When popular or powerful people engage in less-than-wholesome activities or brazenly engage in sinful activities, these actions are glamorized and are used to pull on the emotions of the public, thus belittling or ignoring the truth of the situation—that it is *wrong*!

"Children" Includes Boys

According to *The Gleaner* (Jamaica) article titled "Women Shouldn't Lower Standards For Men – Students" dated November 15, 2012, the Economic and Social Survey showed that most of those dropping out of school and being incarcerated today are boys. It stated, "The survey also shows that of the 1,937 persons who entered correctional institutions in Jamaica last year, males accounted for 1,748 or 90 per cent of that number."

Clearly, the boys are being neglected by the society in general. The men were created as the covering for the females; so as a result, they are open to more direct attacks to destroy them. If they go to prison or are slaughtered, then the society becomes imbalanced.

In the classrooms, there is a female-teacher majority, and they teach both boys and girls. Within a society, it is the man/father who ought to carry out the discipline within the family. Herein lies the problem: there are very few men to help maintain and execute the disciplining and to deal with male-specific issues when they arise. Today, more males are being raped and abused in the society—some experience this from an early age. Then, instead of dealing with the issues on both sides and bringing balance to the situation overall, there is greater focus on the issue of gender—women and girls—than there is on making the society safe for boys *and* girls to live, learn, and grow.

There are often discussions on the issue of Women and Children, but as it concerns the issue of "children," it usually focuses on girls and neglects the boys within the society; but "children" includes boys too. If that neglect continues, then where are the girls going to get husbands—or is that the plan? Furthermore, we cannot exclude the fathers; good ones still exist.

Communication

If we are going to change the society, then we will need to change what we are putting out in the environment—both local and global media will need revamping and added value to their public offerings. Many of the media houses are focusing on the dollar value and the negative things. For example, sex sells! Conflict grabs attention! Disrespect and dishonor are revered! But all these are negatively impacting on the economy, the social fabric of the nation, and are destroying our children.

Some media houses and production companies are not even supporting or producing programs that are family-oriented. Sadly, fabricated "reality" shows are taking over the networks.

Some don't even believe that God is necessary to the environment and in our daily affairs. The general view and perception of the Church and the Holy Scriptures are that those in the Church are money-hungry simpletons who are oblivious to the issues at hand and that the Bible is irrelevant.

The media has a mandate to bring positive changes globally. Negative words shape, change, or bring down a society (James 3:5–11; Isaiah 52:7; Philippians 4:8).

Help Our Children

The continued rape, kidnapping, and murder of our children, not just locally but worldwide, must be a concern for all members of society. There needs to be a stronger outcry from the peoples of the nation, particularly from the businesspeople, the politicians, and the media.

Our children are the future! There is greatness within each of them—not just as future lawyers and doctors but as teachers and problem solvers of every kind! God is the One Who chose who their parents were to be, how they would look, and where they are born—both in terms of lineage and geographical location!

Their assignments and purpose in life are given even before birth. Isaiah 49:1, 5 say, "Listen, O coastlands, to Me, and take heed, you peoples from afar! The LORD has called Me from the womb; from the matrix of My mother He has made mention of My name . . . and now the LORD says, Who formed Me from the womb to be His Servant, to bring Jacob back to Him, so that Israel is gathered to Him (For I shall be glorious in the eyes of the LORD, and My God shall be My strength)." (See also Galatians 1:15; Jeremiah 1:5.)

We need to realize and understand that there are influences that want to destroy our children to get fame and power, to terminate purposes and assignments, and to maintain the old status quo (Exodus 1; Matthew 2).

All parents must know that children are "heritage from the Lord, and the fruit of the womb is a reward . . ." They are not mistakes!

When God gives us children, spiritually or biologically, we are held responsible for their upbringing, provision, protection, and nurturing; they are the ones who will stand in the gates in the future and bring change to the justice system (Psalm 127:3–4).

The Church must also understand that the children are not the least in the church; they are the most important. They are the links to continuity; therefore, most of the funding needs to go to the development of the children and the youth groups.

Both political and businesspersons need to channel more funding to the youth programs, agencies, and groups. They must recognize that their children are not the only ones who need to be exposed to the best of anything!

What We Need to Do

- Parents must be sensitive to the children when they get dreams and visions. They are not "psycho," and it's not because they ate late. God gives different types of dreams and visions to warn, direct, confirm, impart, save lives, and remove pride (Matthew 2:13; Daniel 4:19–37; Joel 2:38).
- Parents need to know the whereabouts of their children at all times, and they also need to know who their friends are and how

to contact their parents. Parents should not send their children on the street to beg and should teach them not to eat from just anybody.

- Communities should ensure that they know their new neighbors. When you know who is in your community, you can better protect your neighborhood and the children.
- Pray for their protection daily. Donate to the Lord via your church for their protection, and as you pray daily, ask the Lord to put a hedge of protection around your children (Job 1:5, 10; 1 Samuel 1:4; Psalm 91).
- Teachers must be more sensitive to discern when a child is experiencing problems at home.
- The Jamaica Constabulary Force should restructure and improve their children and community divisions and deal more specifically with the abused, raped, murdered, and missing children. They should use one of their senior officers working along with the military intelligence, Christian psychologists, and God-fearing forensics personnel.
- The media needs to become aggressive in following the stories that deal with the brutal abuse and slaying of the nation's children. They need to hunt the details of such stories and "dig" to the root to help bring justice to such matters. Oftentimes, such issues are left hanging in the wind if it's no longer a hot topic.

We Must Protect Our Children

With regard to the recent exposing of information by the media concerning the long-standing abuse of our children, I want to congratulate those media representatives for bringing to the fore a pertinent issue that needs to addressed with great fervency. However, we need further investigation and information from the media, particularly targeting the places of influence where such long-standing abuse is generated.

To protect our children, we need to look at every level of the society. Our music and the marketing companies, for example, must be addressed, as it has become the norm that every advertisement and every song that tops the charts contains serious sexual connotations. This occurs in almost every genre of music. What are they telling our children to do?

Another measure we need to put in place to protect our children is a national identification card for them. This card should be requested of each child if they attempt to purchase alcohol, cigarettes, and even lottery tickets! Furthermore, parents must stop sending children to purchase such items.

Many young girls within the inner city communities get pregnant at an early age—under the age of sixteen—and sometimes the parents are fearful of reporting it to the police because the fathers are either dons or some kind of gang member.

We are pushing for casino-style gambling to be at the forefront of the economic recovery program, and these are places that media is going to be given free access. But at what cost are we pushing for this to enter our country? What about the other activities that are taking place behind the scenes that are synonymous with casino-style gambling? These activities that will ultimately engulf our children; what are we going to do about that?

When this high level of sexual child abuse is happening, we need to begin to look at the spiritual aspect of the problem. We need to ask the question a spiritual standpoint—why is this happening?

We need to recognize and understand that when rape, murder, incest, and abuse are taking place on a large scale, it means that something has gone wrong in the nation spiritually, and a door was opened long before to cause this to take place within the nation. Remember King David and Bathsheba? When King David committed adultery with Bathsheba, that opened the door for rape, murder, and incest to enter through his administration and family, because as a result of their actions, there was rape and incest (Amnon, his son, raped his sister; 2 Kings 11), conspiracy, and murder (through his son Absalom).

Are we willing and ready to deal with the issue of common-law relationships (shacking up)? These days it is called "having a life partner." There are a number of influential persons who are not setting good examples by this lifestyle they have chosen. What examples are we setting—spiritually and temporally—for our children?

Suggestions for Solutions

Parents need to be more sensitive to their children. Talk to them and watch their movements. Watch when their grades are falling, and don't just say, "I was like that too." Carry out medical examinations annually.

Choose wisely concerning the Church, doctors, and schools you will send your children.

Instruct your children not to eat from just anyone. Tell them not to sit in anyone's lap except yours. Tell them to come to you if anyone touches them in off-limit areas. Watch their behavior around other family members.

Monitor the social networks and websites they enter, and ensure you know those passwords. Monitor the Internet-ready phones you gave them.

Keep them away from parks with nude sculptures and from shows and concerts with music that have heavy sexual connotations and explicit lyrics.

Schools need to carry out in-depth interviews for all teachers and coaches to the point of checking criminal records. It means that the police personnel have to be well trained and properly equipped to handle such sensitive matters and have to be confidential and respectful to victims, and the information they have concerning such issues have to be properly recorded, updated, and accessible for persons who need to do criminal checks.

Once abuse takes place, then we must keep in mind that both victim and offender need help! The law is not and cannot be the only remedy applied.

Our children are valuable, and we need to protect them to the uttermost!

CHAPTER 17

YOUTH OF THE NATION ARISE!

The latest statistics both locally and internationally regarding the youth and unemployment shows the failure of leadership past and present—within the Church, as well as the civic, business, and political arenas—to create a strong future for the youth. When a country borrows millions in funding to fix roads and other infrastructure, while our youth remain unemployed and in dire need of training at all levels, schooling, help as well as serious attention, direction, and guidance, then, truly, the leadership at every level is without vision. The time has come for those without vision to step aside.

Each time global change is going to take place, God always looks to the youth. Sadly, many nations neglect them and miss the potential embedded within them. The unemployment and hopelessness now being experienced on the global level are the result of a lack of succession and strategic plans to elevate the youth.

The generation that is currently in positions of power within the nations is extremely selfish—intellectually and otherwise—and has robbed the youth worldwide of the opportunities to be all they can be and do for global development and growth. Many of the older generation don't believe the youth are capable because they don't see the young people doing things and thinking in a way they believe it should be done. So they refuse to release the reins to them!

They have put the youth in a difficult position where they have set no proper foundation or examples for them to build on or to follow. The youth today now have to seek Divine guidance so they can know how to build and how to carry a vision for the next generation. They will have to disregard the examples of extreme selfishness and acts of greed and manipulation and follow the example of David in the Bible. If our youth want to be effective and want to see positive development and growth within their nation, they can't walk the path of the forefathers. They will have to walk away from the beliefs, attitudes, strategies, philosophies, and religiosities of this generation of Sauls and stand like David!

They will also have to be bold in confronting the Goliaths and the mountains of debt, crime, violence, immorality, hopelessness, and loss! They have to think outside the box for change, and they cannot carry any baggage! They will now have to learn how to be shepherds and how to care for the people! They will have to learn how to deal with resentment, jealousy, and envy being entertained by older, ritualistic leaders who don't want to give up power.

They must learn to overcome the internal foes first before they learn to deal with the external ones. The internal foes are the Philistines.

Youth, Be Vigilant!

Youth, you must be vigilant! Learn to discern by first cultivating a relationship with the Creator—God. Stay away from false doctrines – New Age doctrines, Scientology, Atheism—and stay away from immorality.

You now have the task of ensuring that righteousness is restored within the nation and that the reproach—which has come through disobedience—is removed.

Youth, ensure that you forgive all those who have afflicted you in your time of preparation and use it as knowledge and wisdom gained.

Ensure that you don't embrace the "strange woman"—she will ravish you! The "strange woman" refers to false doctrines and idol worship. Rejoice with the "wife of your youth." The "wife of your youth" refers to

God's/Godly foundation. Do not forget God, Who is the Author of all your blessings.

"Let no man despise your youth . . ." (1 Timothy 4:12). That means, don't allow the negative words spoken about you as a young person seeking to do the right thing in the sight of God, or what people think about your ability or skill to accomplish certain things for God, stop you from achieving what you need to for and through Him.

Recognize that the things youth have to endure because of the selfishness of a generation should be used as training. These are the bears and lions they are fighting that will remove the pride, ego, and selfishness from you.

Youth, remember that you have the resources, regardless of how small it is or may seem, that will feed and strengthen a nation. Just as it was with the boy who had five loaves and two fishes, which, when brought before the Lord, were used to feed the multitude that was present!

Youth, never sell your birthright—which is your spiritual inheritance—for material things!

Get ready for the change! It is your time *now*!

Whom Should You Trust

There has been great compromise by many of the past generation that has put our youth of today and tomorrow in a compromising situation. The innocence of our youth has been met with the continued deceptions spewed out by the influencers before them and that has set them on a path that is less than desirable for their future.

It is the responsibility of parents to leave an inheritance for their children for continuity and to help to make life easier for them. There is no inheritance for our youth today for tomorrow; the only thing that is being left for them is debt! (Proverbs 13:22).

The politicians have failed to leave an inheritance for the people. They were more focused on building up their own little inheritances and trying to outdo each other—trying to see who can serve longer and who can leave their "legacy" for the history books.

The scripture 1 Corinthians 2:9 says, "But as it is written: 'Eye has not seen, nor ear heard, nor have entered into the heart of man the things which God has prepared for those who love Him.'" It is critical that our youth begin to ask God to open their eyes to know and embrace the things that are freely given to them. This is how we will receive our inheritance.

There is now a conflict between the spirit of the world and the Spirit of God. The spirit of the world brings us in bondage and oppression and is controlled by man's wisdom, man's intellect, man's philosophy, man's ideologies, and man's doctrines to control the masses! God's Spirit liberates you and opens your eyes to the truth, and only through God's Spirit can your eyes be open to see the truths and the deceptions. The spirit of the world promotes carnality and immorality. It opposes God's Spirit and promotes all kinds of doctrines to enslave mankind. What it wants to do is to promote a society free from all religions and show a false path to prosperity—in other words, attempting to get the benefits of God without yielding to His rule.

Ecclesiastes 9:13–15 says, "This wisdom I have also seen under the sun, and it *seemed* great to me: *There was* a little city with few men in it; and a great king came against it, besieged it, and built great snares around it. Now there was found in it a poor wise man, and he by his wisdom delivered the city. Yet no one remembered that same poor man."

The wealthier the politicians get, the poorer the people become; and the poorer the people become, the greater the manipulation of the people. When people are poor, they and their ideas are despised. When a rich fool speaks, it makes headlines!

Every leader must learn from Solomon. He asked God for the wisdom of God to lead! Wisdom is the power to see and the inclination to choose. Every young person must learn that. Many are trying to obtain wisdom but through the wrong source. Not every fruit will make one wise; some are forbidden, and whatever is forbidden cannot make one wise. Wisdom is not knowing good *and* evil; wisdom is knowing good *from* evil.

Wisdom can only come through God. If we all begin to look deeply, we will see politicians globally endorsing each other, because even the very enemies are coming together to distribute the limited resources among themselves.

One of the things about Jesus is that His whole focus is to empower mankind and to restore what rightfully belonged to them. He builds people instead of the edifices, because building infrastructure rather than the people is only preparing them for enslavement—proven by the Egyptians who enslaved the Israelites. It is for this reason also that the banks are taking our own money and then charging us for it!

They will give mortgages and loans but miss two payments, and you will see who owns that house. They have two sets of rules—one for the rich and one for the poor. The poor man is governed by credit and high interest rates if the credit is no good. The rich only need to make a telephone call and debt disappears!

We now have less and less viable opposition globally. Most of them are now dreaming about rising to power simply to get their piece of the wealth; they don't care about much else! We are now headed for that one world government.

If the people truly want freedom and change, they have to change first. We cannot allow persuasive words and eloquent speeches to tickle our ears. Furthermore, the media needs to be less shallow and go deeper.

Life Is More than Sex and Money

Each time there is a generational shift within the earth, the youth always come under attack! Everything comes against the youth. Past generations have failed the youth, and their main recommendations are to engage in immorality or to immerse oneself in drugs!

All young people must recognize that they must make decisions that will help them progress rather than hinder them!

The key to progress and an extended life is the word "honor"! Honor your parents (regardless of their status), honor God, and follow instructions—morning, noon, or night! Your parents are qualified to teach you regardless of their academic qualifications!

Youth, you are under authority, and this is the first government to which you are exposed. The government of the family is designed to be an imitation of the government of God.

FAMILY, THE FIRST LINE OF GOVERNMENT

When we see the youth not giving honor to the government of family, it is a reflection of the nation's response to the government of God; it means the nation is not honoring God either. Breakdown of the family government is a reflection of the breakdown of the government of God in a nation also.

Man cannot bring deliverance to creation unless he is himself delivered. When man falls, it affects creation, and all the negative things affecting creation right now fall right back to man. Man must first change if we want to experience global change.

Youth, don't make permanent decisions based on your temporary situation. Don't allow your emotions to lead you. Value your virtues!

Place value on your virginity. Remember, sex is a God-given gift that allows us to experience as God did—the creation of life and the joy that comes with birthing another human being. All improper sexual activity was seen as an affront to God and lowering of human dignity.

Youth, don't let anybody give you money so that you can be an experimental guinea pig! Study history! See the past mistakes made by others. Understand that many out there are looking out for themselves and want to use you as a platform without regard for what happens to or becomes of you! Be wise!

Youth, stay away from drugs, guns, and marijuana! Think about what you are doing and how it will affect your future—because you have a future! Many will want to tell you that these things are OK and would never tell that to their own children, but because you are not their children, they tell you what they want you to hear! Don't believe the hype!

Stay away from tattoos! Tattoos are not of God, and they are permanent! When things and circumstances change, you can't remove it! Some of you tattoo the names of your boyfriend or girlfriend on yourself, and when it's over, you can't remove it! Then when it's time to marry the real one, you live to regret getting the tattoo in the first place! You are not an animal for branding! Your value is greater!

Youth, get an education! You don't need to have two, three, or four children now! Wait and complete your education. No one can take your education from you once you've got it! Don't allow yourself to be robbed of something so valuable!

Youth, come off the Instagram and get a plan! Upload a solid education because it is going to require dedication, and there is no greater frustration than a man without a plan and life gone wrong!

The same people you are sexting with are the same ones who will ignore you on the street when they have achieved and you have not! And they are not going to take you home to mama!

Youth, recognize that the ones who encourage you to lower your values and your value only want the prize without the package! Don't lower your values or your standards—you are a complete deal, and God made you *priceless*!

There are many out there who walk in fame and fortune, and they want to be a big influence in your lives. But they are often one way before you and another when no one is looking! Beware of the deception!

Youth, develop a good, healthy relationship with God and let Jesus be the center of your lives! Have good manners and respect the elderly; these things will bring you far in life! Help those who need help without looking for something in return! Take care of those younger than you and look out for their best interests too! Remember that what you do today will affect your tomorrow! Let it be positive.

Protect the Youth, Reject Prostitution

A 2001 study funded by the International Labor Organization–International Program on the Elimination of Child Labor (ILO–IPEC) found that children as young as ten years old were actively engaged in prostitution, catering to tourists, strip clubs, and massage parlors.

The economic difficulties and social pressure contribute to the prevalence of child prostitution. The only area of true growth that we have seen in the past twenty-two and a half years under both administrations is the increase in prostitution. Most of our hotels—because of financial constraints—are developing new packages that facilitate the child sex trade under the guise of professional or business class services. Some offer this VIP service on the basis of helping them de-stress from the current economic situation or offering entertainment.

While the law of the land must be obeyed, it is absolutely ironic that there are costly efforts to remove from the sidewalk the "little man" (who doesn't have a proper permit) selling his biscuits and juice to support his family. When they are removed, they migrate to the areas of the nation where they can access the money they need, and, sadly, prostitution is their solution. So while we are attempting to fix one problem and cut down crime and make Jamaica more palatable for tourists, we have in fact shifted the problem to another section on the society, creating an even greater problem for ourselves.

Check the classified section of the national publications, and you will see the extent to which prostitution has saturated the nation. It is even more ticklish because most of those involved are the "elite" of the society.

The Positives and Negatives of Prostitution

The only seemingly positive aspect of prostitution is increased revenue for those engaged in or supporting it.

The negatives include but are not limited to

- increase in the spread of HIV and other STDs;
- increase in divorces and family breakups;
- increase in abortion;
- increase in absentee fathers;
- reduction of life expectancy;
- increase in the number of missing children;
- increase in sexual immorality; and
- increase in the number of pedophiles and other undesirables entering the country.

Economic Reform and Job Creation

What more will it take for the politicians, the business sector, and the church to see that we are going in the wrong direction? It is causing great humiliation on the nation! Do we want more countries to impose visas on Jamaica because of our economic situation and wrong policies before we wake up? They ignore helping the small businesses in employing more people; they are more interested in helping the foreigners who are not keeping the money in the country! We are going after the foreign exchange, and this increases its demand! When this happens, demand for foreign exchange increases, which makes them increase the cost of the foreign exchange and put us in a deeper economic rut.

Solutions

Why not . . .

- host school and summer school programs to encourage the students to become young writers? This would also help them to understand the English language better and help them improve in English literature, thereby allowing for greater passes in these subjects. It will also help those in the universities majoring in journalism and communication to find jobs and get the necessary experience.
- provide special advertising rates to participating companies whether large or small such as discounts and for longer contracts that will attract an even bigger discount?
- visit homes within the inner city and rural areas to deliver newspapers free for a month and sponsor children within these homes whether or not they are in school?
- host fund-raising events for children in inner city and rural areas?
- through government programs, develop free and public training seminars to help jobless inner-city residents? To cut costs and to show that they care, the government officials and members of the opposition should employ their own skills and teach these seminars.
- furthermore, have all inner-city residents and prominent businesspersons make an effort to renew their minds so that "uptown" employers can be more confident in employing inner-city job seekers?

CHAPTER 18

ABORTION ON DEMAND

Everything today is market driven. Decisions are made based on the needs of the market.

Abortion and immorality are now in great demand. Abortion negatively affects business. If population decreases, so will demand for goods and services, including real estate, loans, clothing, food, medical services, and vehicles; thus, population and demand are positively related.

Abortion is affecting the population growth. We are now seeing it negatively affect real estate and other businesses. When the family decreases, it affects the demand for certain kinds of properties. Furthermore, it can significantly change the landscape of the construction industry.

Almost every organization uses market trends to make business decisions, and most businesspersons are now jumping on the bandwagon because, to them, there is a great change toward people who want to engage in abortions, witchcraft, and immorality.

Media and government are also heavily involved in the change in market trends, and their decisions are based on "current trends." As a result, they are also going with the flow of the tide. There is no longer accountability or new ideas, and as such, the words for the moment are "Let's give the people what they want." On that basis, politicians are no longer being held accountable. What is going to happen when the current trend changes? Isn't one of life's constants change?

The Threat of Abortion and Immorality

Abortion and immorality are threats to humanity, while many companies within the various industries will benefit from this trend—pharmaceutical industry, medical industries, the gaming industries, politicians, activists, and the entertainment industry.

Abortion eliminates the true visionaries, geniuses, and those with solutions for the problems that are inevitable. This creates a global vacuum and is a threat to Christianity.

Here's a thought: If other religions don't accept abortion, but Christians and the Christian nations do, what will that do to Christianity and the Christian population? Or is that the plan? In addition to this, studies have shown that most of the abortions that take place are done by black people. Many of the places that conduct abortions are within or close to black communities. Do the checks. Could this be an effort to significantly diminish the black race? Why is abortion being pushed as an alternative for family planning, for developing nations? It is interesting that many of our top athletes and game changers come from developing nations. What is to become of the global society if abortion becomes the order of the day?

Our universities have now become the testing labs and "porn shops" for those testing "market theories" and needing guinea pigs for their experiments. The universities that ought to be churning out the leaders of tomorrow have become the launch pad for immorality, lewd behavior, and less-than-desirable attitudes.

Many have come forward to declare that the people should make their own decisions about their own bodies. This is somewhat a deception. First and foremost is the fact that our bodies are God's property. Our bodies are the temple of the Holy Spirit and, as such, should be respected and treated the way He sees fit. Additionally, Psalm 127:3–4 says, "Children are a heritage from the Lord." Regardless of the way in which they have come about, some children may be unplanned, but they are not unwanted. They are the next Prime Minister, the next beauty queen, and the next track legend!

The Bible describes anything that has blood as having life. By day twenty-two of pregnancy, a fetus' heart begins to beat with its own blood! By the time most women realize they are pregnant, the heart of their fetus is beating, and it means it has life! Research shows approximately ten percent of all legal abortions end with one or more of the following complications: accidental tearing, tearing of the cervix, perforation of the uterus, heavy bleeding, miscarriage of future pregnancies, increased risk of subsequent tubal pregnancies, damage of internal organs, hepatitis, blood clots, sterility, and death. This does not include the psychological effects that abortion can have on those involved.

Let's save the next generation!

Abortion Creating a Global Vacuum

Globally, we are crying out for visionaries and righteous leaders in various sectors to solve the issues that now exist globally. But most of the problems that need to be solved globally have occurred as a result of the vacuum created by abortion. God created each person to bring solutions to issues that He knew would arise as a result of man's selfishness.

As is revealed in the scriptures Jeremiah 1:5, Galatians 1:15, and Psalm 139:13, God's purpose and assignments begin once there is conception.

The issue of therapeutic/elective abortion is an issue that is quite controversial today. Many say it is a woman's right for her to determine what she wants to do with her own body—this is exactly the kind of deception that is running rampant throughout nations.

The scripture 1 Corinthians 6:18–20 reminds us that the Holy Spirit dwells in our bodies, which is His temple. Abortion destroys your physical and spiritual bodies and has the potential to cause great emotional and spiritual damage in the future. In the same way that when the natural laws are broken there are legal consequences, when Spiritual Laws are broken, it opens the door for other things to happen personally and in the wider society.

Today we are seeing the residual effects of abortion as it affects our nations. How so? Abortion opens the door to untimely deaths, violence, crime, as well as the eradication of purpose, vision, and ideas for all sectors.

From the beginning of time, everything we do individually affects the world entirely. Our personal choices have caused climate changes, environmental shifts, increased deaths, diminished values, and so much more (Genesis 3:17). When we think that we are getting rid of a potential problem, we are in fact creating bigger ones.

What if the purposes of certain well-known people in the numerous sectors were never brought to light because of abortion? What if the great men and women of the past and of today who were raised by single parents never existed because of abortion? What if there was no Bob Marley, Martin Luther King Jr., or Nelson Mandela? We would never have the benefit of their gifts, talents, and expertise, and whatever impact they have made would never have been!

Some nations are using legislation to force women to abort their girls. What if the nations did not have the benefit of some of the great women of the past and present? What if there was no Florence Nightingale, Marie Curie, or Mother Teresa? All these women contributed immensely to sensitizing the nations to issues such as poverty, health, justice, and science, and made significant impact on global laws and economies.

What Nations Should Do

Reduce the funds/funding being spent on abortions and give those to humanitarian groups and NGOs who will educate, empower, and enrich the lives of the poor and neglected ones worldwide.

Relax adoption laws that hinder those who genuinely qualify to keep the children who are unwanted by their natural parents. Help those who want to adopt, regardless of their income level, to do so and make a positive difference in the lives of the unplanned children. It should not be easier to abort a child rather than to adopt one! It's not right.

In a study done by the United States in 2012, the following was revealed:

- Fifty percent of US women obtaining abortions are younger than twenty-five; women aged twenty to twenty-four obtain 33 percent of all US abortions, and teenagers obtain seventeen percent.
- In 2009, adolescents under fifteen years obtained 0.05 percent of all abortions but had the highest abortion ratio, 785 abortions for every 1,000 live births.
- Black women are more than 4.8 times more likely than non-Hispanic white women to have an abortion, and Hispanic women are 2.7 times as likely.
- In 2009, 85 percent of all abortions were performed on unmarried women.
- Among women who obtained abortions in 2009, 40.2 percent had no prior live births, 46.3 percent had one or two prior live births, and 13.6 percent had three or more prior live births.

If this is so for one nation, what is happening in your nation under your noses—without our knowledge? What valuable resources are the nations—and even our own lives—lacking when abortions are performed?

Food for thought.

CHAPTER 19

STAND IN THE GAP FOR THE NEXT GENERATION

Ezekiel 22:30 says, "So I sought for a man among them who would make a wall, and stand in the gap before Me on behalf of the land, that I should not destroy it; but I found no one."

Many times, people will criticize the Church and ask what they are doing about the negative happenings within a nation or the world. But we must recognize that we are the Church—every profession—and we have a responsibility individually and collectively to stand in the gap for nations. We have become a nation of people that have become caught up in our own little issues/problems/situations, forgetting that we also have a duty to each other and to our nation. Some are so caught up in showing off their latest "self-improvement" projects—who has the latest clothes or enhanced body parts—and when tragedy strikes then is when they get concerned.

When negative happenings begin—murder, rape, and famine—and then hopelessness sets in, it means that there is a break/breach within the spiritual walls of the nation. If someone breaks into a home, if the owner simply adds a burglar alarm without fixing the breach—the broken window/door—then their efforts are wasted. Hence, God wants persons of every profession at every level to make themselves available to Him to be used to rebuild the walls—not the physical but the spiritual walls. We need to "stand in the gap."

Standing in the gap is a metaphor for committed intercession. When there is a gap between man and God, someone needs to stand in and intercede so that God can repair the breach for us. Hence, we have a responsibility to first identify the breach in every profession and stand in.

When there is a breach in the walls, everything comes in—anything takes place. If we are looking for restoration of the family, a good justice system, good governance, and healing within a nation, then it is the responsibility of everyone to stand in the gap that the spiritual barriers will be rebuilt. Regardless of the systems or laws put in place, no change will come if there is a gap in the wall.

Every Profession

To be effective, every profession knows its own terminologies and jargon and, so, knows the precise words to use as opposed to the ordinary layperson who would not be as knowledgeable in that area. For example, a lawyer knows the jargon and terms that he/she would use for certain matters, like "petition," "counter petition," "recuse," "abrogate," so they could pray accordingly, employing those terms that John Q. Public would not ordinarily know. People who deal with the economy of a nation need to stand in the gap for the things of that industry that are affecting the nation—inflation, devaluation of the dollar, fiscal policies, and so on. They know the terminologies to use as they pray to stop the negative and ask for the increase of the positive. Doctors would know the diseases that are plaguing the nation and would pray accordingly for them to stop using medical terminologies. They would stand in the gap to minimize sicknesses and diseases that are eating away the nation—cancer, HIV, and others—and that God will release medical breakthroughs to heal the nation. Security forces also need to stand in the gap; they can't simply focus on the physical but also the spiritual aspect.

Interestingly, there is a name of God—a name ascribed to God that represents every one of these industries in our society.

Effective intercession brings change within a nation, but each person who stands in the gap must realize that we cannot operate the same way that we operated twenty years ago. Twenty years ago, we did not have the technological revolution we now have, and now as knowledge has increased, so has the technological warfare. There are now games and software that are designed to pollute the minds of our youth and encourage them to commit crimes and do other things, and this is a breach. We need people to rise up in the information technology arena to use the relevant jargon and references as they stand in the gap and fight for our young people and the future of the nation.

Recognize that the mind and eyes are direct links to the soul, and, as such, whoever will control the mind and eyes will control the next generation.

It is the responsibility of every profession to stand in the gap that change will take place.

REAL TALK
ABOUT SEX

CHAPTER 20

GOOD MARRIAGE, GOOD SEX—BLESSINGS FROM GOD

God wants married couples to enjoy sex within the boundaries described in His Word. But this is an area where many struggle and are in fact attacked because they deem this area private.

There are many forces that come against a married couple's sex life—exes and jealous individuals who will speak negatively against a person's sex life for there to be frustration and failure in that area.

A good marriage and a good sex life bring better governance. In the same way that there are prayers and teachings regarding money and healing, there are prayers and teachings that we must engage in concerning sex and marriage, and Christians must be taught on their value and importance.

There are too many problems and scandals taking place in the lives of politicians, pastors, musicians, and worship personnel; not to mention the pain and turmoil in their private lives. Some are deceived by the enemy about their sexual identity and orientation. We need more deliverance ministers to rise up within the church and take a stand against these forces of darkness that are coming against God's people.

There is too much emphasis being placed on financial prosperity and even prophetic ministry, while many ignore conferences and seminars to help those struggling in this area.

People are spending millions of dollars going to rehab only to become worse. There is nothing that the power of God cannot do, including

- breaking un-Godly soul ties; and
- giving tactics and strategies on how to fight and overcome.

Sex is important. If it was not important, so much money wouldn't be pumped into destroying sex lives.

There are so many un-Godly devices being advertised—all of which are artificial; in addition to the swing clubs and gentlemen's clubs, enhancement drugs are being pushed and sold at high prices, causing great damage.

The Sex Industry is a $97 billion industry—that alone will tell you what is happening.

It is time for the Church to rise up and utilize the God-given wisdom, including revelation, and herbal remedies that God has created to help us.

In 1 Corinthians 7:1–5, Paul outlined the importance of marriage and sex. He outlined to us that we should not fast for long periods because it would bring temptation so that sexual immorality takes place. He also outlined that one should not withhold sex from his/her partner—people are doing this with their spouses for money or other reasons.

Satan hates God's people—especially those who are married. People should fight for their sex lives—it should never be a burden. There are many things the enemy has put in place to destroy the sex lives and intimacy of married couples. On this note, recognize that the flexi-work week is the enemy of good marriages and sex lives. Employment today is also taking a toll on the sex and family lives. Some persons have been manipulated to engage in sexual immorality to keep their jobs.

It would be a good idea for the hotel industry to start giving big discounts to married couples, especially for vacations and vow renewals. This will increase vitality and reduce infidelity. Remember, sex is a gift from God that He placed in human beings for pleasure and procreation.

The scripture 1 Corinthians 6:16–20 says, "Or do you not know that he who is joined to a harlot is one body with her? For 'the two,' He says, 'shall become one flesh.' But he who is joined to the Lord is one spirit with Him. Flee sexual immorality. Every sin that a man does is outside the body, but he who commits sexual immorality sins against his own body. Or do you not know that your body is the temple of the Holy Spirit who is in you, whom you have from God, and you are not your own? For you were bought at a price; therefore glorify God in your body and in your spirit, which are God's."

Spice It Up!

Good sex reduces stress and worry, and brings peace and joy. There are various fragrances, food, fruits, nuts, soups, and drinks (non-alcoholic) that can make the sexual experience most enjoyable and exciting.

This is a declaration that every wife needs to declare regularly, if not daily.

Songs of Solomon 4:16 says, "Awake, O north wind, And come, O south! Blow upon my garden that its spices may flow out. Let my beloved come to his garden and eat its pleasant fruits."

Prayer for Your Sex Life

Father, in the name of Jesus, we put our sex life under the Blood of Jesus. Every un-Godly soul tie and every satanic altar erected to destroy my sex life, we break them down now in the name of Jesus. Every negative word that has been spoken against my sex life to shut down my body, we break it in the name of Jesus. We ask You, Lord, to touch our minds, bodies, and our souls. Every organ will work perfectly; our blood will flow perfectly. We thank You, Holy Spirit, that You are the Creator of Life and that You desire that Your people have good sex lives. Bind the strongman and break the strongholds and cut all connecting chords and break tiredness and lethargy. Let witchcraft become powerless. We thank You, Lord, for a good sex life. Amen.

CHAPTER 21

SPICE UP YOUR SEX LIFE

S ex is a topic that a lot of people are afraid to talk about, but a part
of the prosperity that God has for mankind is for married couples to
enjoy good sex. God created natural things in the earth for mankind
for sustenance of sex life. You don't need to take drugs to spice up your
sex life; neither do you need to use artificial stimulators or try X-rated
stuff to spice up your sex life. There are many tools and toys made these
days that are said to enhance people's sex life, but that is a deception.
Instead, they destroy their sex lives and ultimately their relationships.
Just as we commit our lives to God, we must ask God also to bless our sex
lives. One does not have to try yoga, meditation, or masturbation to spice
up their sex life. There are many ways God can help married couples
through difficult times in this area.

Understand that there are persons out there, whether they are past
lovers or persons who are envious or jealous of your marriage, who will
speak against your sex life because they know that if your sex life suffers,
it can bring frustration and pain and can lead to divorce. Sex in marriage
is a good thing (Genesis 1:27–28; Genesis 2:24; Genesis 5:18–19).

The scripture 1 Corinthians 7:2–3 reveals to us that God wants
married couples to satisfy each other sexually.

The scripture 1 Corinthians 7:5 reminds us to "never deprive each other." It is up to you to ensure that you fulfill your sexual duties to your spouse without complaining. Remember, good sex reduces stress. Declare the Word of God over your life daily to satisfy each other sexually. Ensure that you always create the atmosphere before you have sex romantic candles and music; it is not necessary at that time to play gospel music!

Hebrews 13:4 says, stay away from immorality. Use consecrated olive oil and anoint your sexual areas daily and massage each other regularly.

Look out for those who want to destroy your marriage and watch out for all third-party persons. Watch out for subtle dinner and lunch dates especially at the workplace, and be careful in whom you confide.

Be careful of accepting gifts; these sometimes come with wrong motives. Always remember that the enemy is after Christian marriages, and he hates a good marriage.

Foods That Can Stimulate Your Sex Life

- grapes, apples, melons, banana, pear
- chicken soup
- cornmeal porridge
- pumpkin seed
- fish, barley, pepper
- grape juice and orange juice
- almond milk, honey
- parsley, cinnamon, garlic, ginger (God created these spices to spice up your sex life)
- non-alcoholic wine

*Ensure that you take your sea bath regularly; the salt in the sea will do a lot for you.

Pray About Your Sex Life

Regardless of what you pray for on a daily basis, ensure that you unite and pray for your sex life. Pray this prayer:

Father, in the name of Jesus, I thank You each day, Lord, that You will bless me in the area of sex. Give me the necessary stamina to fulfill my purpose within the bedroom. Help us to satisfy each other and give us stamina, drive, longevity, and compassion for each other. Cover our sex life from attacks and every word spoken from third parties.

(Husband, say) Let the breast of my wife satisfy me.

(Wife, say) Let every touch of my husband satisfy me. Give him skill, tactic, and strategies.

Let us only have desire for each other and help us to have patience with each other. Let there be purity in our sex life. Let us hunger for each other daily, and let each time sex takes place we receive maximum satisfaction. Lord, cover our minds from soul ties and close every portal in our lives that the enemy would use to attack our sex life. We thank you, Lord, that You have blessed us. In Jesus' name. Amen.

Take note:

- Wives, remember always dress sexy for your husband.
- Husbands and wives, be sensitive to each other's needs.

Pray for a Healthy Sex Life

As the institution of marriage continues to come under attack, in particular within the Christian countries, it is the duty of all Christians to pray for God-given illumination. There is a difference between illumination and inspiration. Illumination refers to the influence of the Holy Spirit, which helps Christians to grasp the things of God (1 Corinthians 2:4; Matthew 16:17). All spiritual knowledge must be by revelation.

The Christian marriages are under attack by Canaanite cults. God has given Christians the resource of the Holy Spirit and the Word of God. Christians need to be wary of theologians who want to interpret scripture without a belief in or acceptance of the Holy Spirit! That is very dangerous! Many people are turning away from Christianity because they are tired of religiosity; they want to see the power of God manifest in their lives.

There are three stages of marriage recorded in the Bible that all Christians should know.

1) Contract (Genesis 29:15–20; Genesis 24:33, 51–54, 57–58)
2) Consummation (Genesis 29:21–26; Genesis 24;64–67)
3) Celebration (Genesis 29:27–28)

Once one becomes married, it becomes a contract and a consent to have sex. What happens once the contract is breached—even through withholding sex? (I want to hear what the legal minds have to say about that!)

What happens when a contract is breached? When a contract is breached, it becomes voidable. The party in the right can terminate! Hence, divorce lawyers and the courts will be making a lot of money at the expense of family.

Christian marriages are deemed as covenant marriages! The devil hates it because it becomes a threefold chord, which is not easily broken. What people should be lobbying for, instead, is for laws to be put in place to deal with adultery and fornication, and to deal with those going beyond the scriptural boundaries of marriage, and to ensure that there be restitution, physically and financially, to those they have hurt.

An attack on Christian marriages is ultimately an attack on the Church. When married people engage in sex, it is spiritual warfare against the enemy, because what we are in fact doing is reproducing the image of God in which we were made and procreating as He instructed.

Practical Pointers

1) You must invest in your sex life.
2) Anoint both your and your spouse's sexual areas each day. This is to ensure against premature ejaculation, mind attacks during sex, low feeling, loss of sexual desire for you, losing interest in sex, or witchcraft from people who want to break up your marriage.
3) Good sex brings healing and joy and lets you relax at work and helps you think clearly. This not only supports mental health but is part of prosperity as well.

4) Your sex life is the most important part of the marriage. God wants you to enjoy sex. The enemy does not want you to enjoy it in marriage; he, instead, wants to go after sex in un-Godly relationships using unnatural devices.

5) Ask the Lord to cut off all soul ties with past lovers and free your mind of them and yourself of the feelings! Don't bring the past relationships and issues into the present one.

6) Irish moss, carrot juice, barley, pumpkin seed, soursop, and soursop leaf are good for both you and your spouse! In addition to the nutritional value, these serve to enhance a person's sex life.

7) Drink a lot of water before having sex.

8) Exercise at least twice per week.

9) Play romantic music, particularly the ones you liked when you first met each other.

10) Try different positions, not just the missionary position. And try different places too—your swimming pool, the car, the beach. Variety is the spice of life!

11) Give each other a massage and help each other to relax.

12) Do not allow the children to interfere with your sex life! Send them over to the grandparents for the weekend and go relax at a hotel or enjoy dinner and a movie. In addition to that, good home-cooked chicken soup and a good warm bath also help.

13) Pray the word of God daily to have a successful marriage and a good sex life! Remember that the enemy is working overtime to destroy covenant marriages.

Entrepreneurs: Invest in Your Sex Life!

"A healthy and good sex life is important to every marriage and is a blessing from the Lord! Contrary to popular belief, but in accordance with Biblical Principles, sex is for marriage! Although it is not often discussed and deemed private, a good sex life enhances every other aspect of personal and public life. Below is a list of things to remember that will enhance your sex life!" (*Man, Money, Ministry*, 2010)

FAMILY, THE FIRST LINE OF GOVERNMENT

God's desire for man is that we "prosper and be in good health even as your soul prospers." For most entrepreneurs, this is an area of frustration. While most of them prefer not to talk about it, it affects their business and ultimately the nation, because it affects their decision-making abilities.

Many contracts, business, and national-level decisions take place in the bedroom! Even judicial decisions! Some people are bitter and frustrated. Some have been abused, but because of their positions and status, they are afraid to say it! Some complain that there is a breakdown in the relationship after years of marriage. Others complain that their partners have stopped doing what they used to, to keep them interested. Still others say that having suffered rape and other such abusive experiences, their marriages suffer, too, because it has become a roadblock in the marriage and was never dealt with.

We have seen multimillion dollar company leaders, sports stars, politicians, VIPs, and even religious personnel suffer loss because of this issue.

We must recognize that this is not a natural problem but a spiritual one. It therefore cannot be dealt with through natural therapy. Instead, it has to be dealt with from a spiritual standpoint! It has to be dealt with from the root. Only Jesus Christ can deliver persons from this matter. When it is properly dealt with, millions of dollars can be saved! Additionally, many lives will also be saved, and the nation will experience change for the better.

Many organizations are making millions from the sex trade, and it is now influencing the legislation. It affects the household spending habits because some spouses, when they get paid, have to share their salaries with their wives, husbands, and sweethearts. They often end up neglecting to take care of the needs of their children.

Regardless of the proposed reforms of the private and public sectors, until we deal with the familial and sexual issues afflicting the people of the nation, reforms will fail.

Attacks on the family were among the first economic catastrophes that took place in the Garden of Eden. Family affects both nation and business.

Solutions

First, recognize, understand, and accept the fact that marriage is one of the biggest investments you can make.

- Find out if there is sexual integrity! That is, you must identify whether infidelity exists in the marriage. If there is, then healing and restoration must take place quickly.
- Pray—people pray for everything else except for the healthy sex lives of husbands and wives. We need to pray more aggressively in that area—that husbands and wives have a good, healthy sex life; it is the area of greatest attack.
- Do not allow the children to interfere with your sex life! Send them over to their grandparents for the weekend, and go relax at a hotel or dinner and a movie. (*Man, Money, Ministry*, 2010)
- Cut down on the late work hours, nightclubbing, lengthy studying, and barhopping. Being a professional student also destroys family relationships and marriages. Pastors and other Church leaders often spend too much time with ungrateful Christians while their own families suffer! Military personnel become more involved with their military duties than with their own families, and the relationships break down. Any promotion that is tied to or is as a result of sex is not worth it! It is better to walk away and maintain a healthy marriage and sex life.

The longevity of any organization or nation is determined by the health of the marriages and sex lives of the decision-makers and the people of the nation.

CHAPTER 22

ARE THERE SEXUAL BOUNDARIES?

Sex is a very personal and very sensitive issue, but it is now the number-one issue dominating the globe and affecting areas such as legislation, economy, and education. Not even poverty is as dominant an issue as sex these days. The fact that it is such an issue today makes it less personal and more of a public issue that needs to be addressed so that we can get back to the really pertinent issues.

Oftentimes, the things that we are afraid to discuss are the things that always destroy us. In every setting, if you were to ask who has a financial problem, most, if not all, who are present would stand or raise their hands. But if you were to ask who is having a sexual problem, then nobody would stand, but they would ask to speak to you privately afterward.

The reason the church leaders are not as effective as they ought to be is that the enemy plagues the people with sexual issues, psychological problems, and varying often superstitious beliefs.

Here is an issue: for example—"Is oral sex wrong?"

From a medical perspective, doctors will tell you that it has the potential to cause gonorrhea of the throat, yeast infections, chlamydia, human immunodeficiency virus (HIV), herpes, among other things.

From a spiritual perspective, the mouth is supposed to be a consecrated organ that should speak life, blessings, and positive things (Isaiah 6:4, 7).

Most leaders will use Hebrews 13:4 to justify that married couples can do whatever they want including the oral, anal, or bondage form of intercourse.

Now while most may say this is no else's business but those involved, the scriptures do speak on lawful versus unlawful sex. This particular scripture is showing us that sex outside of marriage, or with whoremongers, adulterers, fornicators, and so on, is defiling and that sex within the confines of marriage (as laid out in the scriptures) was not.

God created male and female married couples to have sex; thus, sexual intercourse glorifies God, our Creator (Genesis 1:27, 31; Proverbs 6:5). God's purpose for sex was for us to reproduce after our kind, with a bonus of experiences such as pleasure, intimacy, spiritual bonding, stress release, and deliverance from temptation.

That being said, having recognized that God created us to have sex to reproduce, how can we reproduce through oral or anal sex?

Interestingly, there was an instance where God struck a man dead for spilling his seed/semen (Genesis 38:9–10).

Proverbs 5:19 states, "As a loving deer and a graceful doe, Let her breasts satisfy you at all times; And always be enraptured with her love."

God wants our sexual needs met but in a way that does not defile; there are boundaries. These boundaries are not physical; they are spiritual and moral. There is no need for sex toys and R or X-rated movies to stimulate any individual. But recognize that each person has a different calling, and wherever the Bible is silent on a particular area, one should seek the Holy Spirit to give them clarity or instruction on the matter. The Holy Spirit is Comforter, Counselor, Advocate and Helper (John 15:26; John 16:5–15).

God wants us to enjoy sex so much that He laid it out in His Word that a husband or wife should not deny either party of this wonderful gift! Husbands and wives should not even go on long fasts to deny each other (1 Corinthians 7:3–5).

Wisdom

When in the scriptures it says that someone "knew" someone, it was not referring to mere acquaintances; it was telling us that someone had intercourse with someone. It is the duty of the husband to take care of his wife generously in this area, and also the duty of the wife to do the same.

If every Pastor, politician, doctor, teacher, lawyer, judge, laborer, journalist, musician, or bus driver would feed their wives sexually as they contribute to or influence the society, then we will see major and positive changes in the society and balance restored!

It is time to pray that your sex life will become hotter and more pleasure-filled. Pray before sex and ask God to strengthen you and grant you more stamina to be a long-distance "runner." Pray that all the forces working against the health of your sex life—your mind, the problems you face, and other things—will go so that you may enjoy the gift He has given you and even cause you to be more creative!

Marital Rape: A Blatant Attack on Christian Principles!

The Bible calls sexual intimacy in marriage a privilege and a mystery by which a man and a woman become one! (Ephesians 5:32; Genesis 2:24). However, the privilege is abused when people who are not married to each other have sexual intercourse (1 Corinthians 5:1; 1 Corinthians 6:16).

Marriage symbolizes the love of Christ for the Church which brings joy and delight, but sex outside of the Biblical boundaries is destructive (1 Corinthians 6:15–16; Proverbs 5:3–11, 15, 18).

The political or social distinction of temporal life is not the most important. What matters is obedience to God. Christians should not change to fit the worldviews. We stand on the view of God!

There are innumerable attacks coming against marriage, and it is all a plan to destroy this Christian principle. It is imperative for Christians to stand and push back any destructive elements. There are all manner of systems and groups put in place to successfully divide the family and break up marriages. They began with the terminology "women and children," while they ignored and neglected the men! They want to shift the consent age to destroy the bodies and derail the emotions of our children.

Let us understand that sexual drive is not a sinful thing. What is sinful is committing the acts of adultery or fornication or going beyond the boundaries of what the Bible outlines.

Married couples should in no way deprive each other of sex! God made it for married people to enjoy and to procreate. The Bible clearly outlines that the only way one would "deprive" the other is if there is mutual consent, and then it would have been agreed upon. Even if as a Christian couple there is fasting but one can't hold out, then the couple should come together and engage in sex.

Many arguments have been surfacing lately about marital rape. There is no such thing as marital rape, and this is a blatant attack on Christian principles.

The scripture 1 Corinthians 7:4 says, "The wife does not have authority over her own body, but the husband *does*. And likewise the husband does not have authority over his own body, but the wife *does*."

Once the man or woman is fit and healthy—there are no negatively impacting health issues—then neither should deny each other of the privilege of sexual intercourse. A lot of persons are pushing different agendas to destroy the principles of marriage; others are speaking from a place of deep hurt and abuse from which they need to be delivered and restored to the point of healing.

God's Word is truth and light! For many, because of the influence of Hollywood and perverted media, there is a push to discredit and destroy this honorable institution of God's gift called Marriage! It is the duty of everyone to pray so that this argument/matter never becomes a reality!

I know of situations where women were influenced by others to hold back sex until the husband pays her separately for the privilege. There are other situations that because the man is going through a financial situation where he could not provide adequately for his family, he was denied of sex. In other cases, some deny their spouse because they were not properly satisfied. Some deny because there is a third party. But regardless of the situation, we have to fast and pray that one's sex life remains intact. Both parties must put away selfishness in marriage and make every effort to satisfy each other!

Why is there so much fight against sex? Today, sex has become more important to many than feeding the homeless!

The Bible says that a person ought not to "burn" but, instead, get married and enjoy the privilege and mystery of sex. While sex is still a temporal arrangement and not a part of our eternal existence, and while marriage itself is an earthly institution—both are equally important, and God honors sex within marital boundaries.

If one is single and does not have the gift of celibacy—doesn't burn with the passion (1 Corinthians 7:7–9)—get married and enjoy all the sex you want!

If the powers that be would invest in going into the communities and encourage our young people—who are being pimped, trafficked, and even abused by influential ones in our society who think they are untouchable—to get married and structure their lives better, then we would see how much it would improve the fabric of our society!

Masturbation Will Pollute Your Mind

Proverbs 16:2 says, "All the ways of a man are pure in his own eyes, but the Lord weighs the spirits."

We are living in a time where many are promoting a society without boundaries, which they call a free society. That means you are free to do whatever you want to do with your body; no moral and social values and no limits. We must remember that we are either a slave to sin or a slave to righteousness. In pursuing freedom, many find themselves in bondage. No one can serve two masters. Masturbation is one such thing that will mess up your mind and your spirit. Our spirit is important. God wants man to be whole—spirit, soul, and body (1 Thessalonians 5:23). When your spirit is polluted, you are not able to discern truth from lies and you make wrong choices/poor decisions and things are done in the wrong spirit, and God wants us to have pure hearts and a right spirit (Psalm 51; Proverbs 20:27). It is sin that has separated man from God, and it destroyed that strong and healthy relationship man had with God. So when your mind is polluted—in the same way that negativity and negative music can pollute one's spirit—it denies you of even your daily benefits and what God has in store for you. God's word says, "As a man thinks, so is he." So when we sing about things that are opposite to the Word and will of God for our lives, then it manifests accordingly. When we begin to speak or sing about "dawgs" and engaging in oral sex or having girls in twos, threes, sevens, and elevens—once the mind is polluted, the manifestation is not far behind. The diversion from the natural purpose of what God intended sex to be will bring pollution especially of the mind and spirit. So as a result of some of that, more families are in turmoil, and we will also see it playing out among our babies in the schools.

Masturbation and the Transfer of Spirits

There is such a thing as transference of spirit—good or bad. In the Bible, when God is going to bless people or have an act of ordination, he instructs that hands be laid upon the people to give them power and that those laying hands have an excellent spirit to carry out the function. What if that leader is masturbating—what will happen? There will be a transfer of an unclean spirit (Numbers 11:16–17; Isaiah 42:5; Zachariah 12:1). What about the person who massages you and does your hair and nails who may be masturbating? There will be a transfer of an unclean spirit to you, and, at some point, you may find yourself doing it too. Your head, feet, hands, eyes, mouth, and sexual organs are gates of the human body/spirit/soul, and they will open the door to other unclean acts. Most people who are involved in masturbation have restless nights in enjoying their sexual relationships with their spouse. It also opens the door for unclean spirits named incubus and succubus that attack them in their dreams, and the result is what many know as wet dreams. In the Bible, when people had this issue, God would instruct them to wash (Leviticus 15:16–17).

People who engage in masturbation will have serious psychological effects, which lead to isolation, abuse, and competing with their spouses. If a person is single, it takes longer to get to the point of marriage, and it would bring serious problems and pain after marriage. Hosea 4:6 says, "My people are destroyed for lack of knowledge . . ."

God made sex, but there are borders and boundaries (Hebrews 13:4). Our bodies are the temple of God; we don't have ownership—we have stewardship. Spiritually, our hands are very important. They represent power, strength, service, oath of allegiance, honor, and worship of God, as well as blessings. It is even critical to know that not everyone should hold or shake your hands. Spiritually and naturally, diseases can be contracted by touching hands. Here's a question: Why would someone masturbate when God has given them a wife/husband?

Sex is good, but beyond the context of what God said, it pollutes us and what God designed for us to be a blessing; we, by our actions, make it a curse. When people are masturbating, they have to think about other people, and so that in itself will pollute your mind especially if you are in a marriage relationship.

CHAPTER 23

TEN MISTAKES MARRIED COUPLES SHOULDN'T MAKE

Family is the first line of government in any society and needs to be properly managed and maintained. When we get marriages to function properly in the society, then other institutions will then function right to make for a better society.

Sadly, the institution of marriage is under serious attack, and the following are things that married couples should avoid doing:

1. *Entertaining division in the vision.* A married couple should not have two different visions and sets of goals especially as it relates to the family unit. They are one. So when God says "leave and cleave," it means that each must put aside anything that would cause them to function as two independent units and embrace what would cause or allow them to function as one strong unit— in sync, fighting for one goal and accomplishing a single purpose for the family unit.

2. *Giving control of your marriage to relatives and friends.* Handing over control of your marriage and decision-making that

takes place within it to family members and friends can cause divorce. When it is time for decision-making at any level within your marriage, you and your spouse should work it out through communication and prayer. If that fails, then seek counseling from qualified persons who also have the best interest of your marriage at heart.

3. *Allowing social networks to steal quality time.* Do not allow social networks/media to rob you of valuable and quality time with your spouse and your family. Hiding passwords from each other, allowing "ex-friends/ex-partners" to give you counsel about your marriage, or posting pictures of past relationships with other friends commenting exposes your family to verbal attacks and can have significant and grave consequences for your marriage and family life.

4. *Deliberately depriving each other of sex.* This is never to be a weapon in your marriage. The Bible is clear on it in 1 Corinthians 7:1–5 and Ephesians 5:22–24. Sex is a part of the covenant ascribed by God to husband and wife married to each other.

5. *Nagging* (Proverbs 21:19). Nagging turns a person off and is an enemy to zeal and enthusiasm. It is defiling. While nagging can be found on both sides, women are often found to be more guilty. Nagging has the potential to drive a husband into the arms of another. Nagging doesn't solve anything; prayer and fasting do!

6. *Poor communication.* A lack of communication is the number-one reason for marriage breakups. Communication is not simply talking with each other; it involves attitudes, mannerisms, body language, and even habits. Non-communication is also a form of communication but at its poorest level. Some spouses make decisions for the family but do not communicate it to the other.

7. Excluding God from your marriage and family relationships. Never make the mistake that society has by excluding God from your family unit. God is to be first in your marriage and in your family unit. Prayer and the Word of God in decision-making must be the first priority! When problems arise, the Word will guide you. A simple thing as going to bed with unresolved problems can become disastrous! (1 Peter 3:7; Ephesians 4:26).

8. *Unforgiveness and not spending enough time together.* Never bring past hurts into your marriage. Focus on the future and not the past. You have to make up your mind to let things of the past go! Spend time doing things together. Marriage is about compromising and giving to and for each other.

9. *Adultery and negative criticism.* Avoid adultery altogether! Never compare your marriage with others. Avoid X-rated movies and pornography as stimulants for your marriage. Furthermore, negative criticism of each other *must* be avoided. Speak life to each other. Stay away from pornography, swing clubs, and yoga.

10. *Neglecting the joys of an exciting sex life.* Change our eating habits and set up a health plan for fitness. Be careful of personal trainers. Engage in healthy weight management together and embrace the use of natural remedies—herbs, fruits, vegetables, and nuts—to help you maintain a healthy and exciting sex life. Get back to basics and enjoy the benefits of these foods that God created, including melons, lettuce, almonds, unsalted peanuts, walnuts, flaxseeds, sesame seeds, and pumpkin seeds, and invest in a good blender or extractor. Ezekiel 47:12 reminds us that the leaves bring healing, and God wants us healed–body, soul, and spirit, and, at the same time, get a revelation of the benefits of the natural gifts He has given us.

The family is under attack, and it is time to fight back!

CHAPTER 24

THE PAIN OF CHEATING

O vercoming cheating/infidelity is not something easy to do or to deal with. With the global economic situation and the various nations and media pushing immorality, the institution of family is in crisis mode. There are many other devices used to promote and propel immorality, including swing clubs, websites, and reality television programs. In recent times, approximately four hundred churches/church personnel were caught employing the use of a website that promotes and engages infidelity.

Cheating is one of the most painful things to deal with because it is perceived as an act of betrayal and trust. Cheating carries consequences—both spiritual and physical. Spiritually, it carries soul ties and opens the door for other tragedies to enter. For example, when David committed adultery, it almost destroyed his entire administration and wreaked havoc in his family.

Why Do People Cheat?

Different statistics show that the numbers for both males and females who cheat are quite close. It went further to reveal that women cheat for emotional reasons, while men cheat for pleasure. In counseling with women, they have shared with me that they like to spend time with their men and they enjoy talking and sharing. For instance, where a woman may speak, for example, one million words for the day, a man may only care to speak five hundred words; hence, that is a part of the frustration.

While the men would want to spend time with the boys engaging in sports and even competitions, the women want to go with them, too—even if they don't understand the game—in an effort to understand the men more or to become more involved in sharing their lives.

The men are quicker to cheat with waitresses, go-go dancers, massage therapists, coworkers, or helpers. Women are quicker to cheat with gym instructors, yoga instructors, coworkers, or neighbors who will spend more time and listen to them. Persons we consider to be VIPs will even choose mates among their bodyguards. In the entertainment industry, actors go with actors and singers go with the dancers. In sports, the sports personalities will go with the cheerleaders. Sadly, church leaders sometimes find themselves in the wrong situation with other leaders or members with whom they spend more of their time.

Cheating affects not only the persons directly involved but also their children, friends, and family members. Over the years, I have seen situations where children are conceived and one tries to hide it to preserve the family, but it still comes to light.

Very often, if the person is influential in society, the media will expose it, especially if he/she is running for office. We are seeing it played out, as an example, in television series such as *The Haves and the Have Nots*.

Ways to Avoid Cheating

There are many things husbands and wives need to do to avoid cheating:

- Exercise trust—share passwords.
- Compliment each other.
- Do not withhold sex from each other.
- Maintain the things you did that brought you together.
- Invest in family time.
- Avoid unnecessary business trips without your spouse. (Most corporations need to allow the spouses to travel with their employees on long-distance business trips.)
- Pray together.
- Cut down on the long hours spent on social media.
- Stay away from pornography of any kind and sex toys.

When cheating takes place, there is always the option of divorce. But before you go that route, always make the effort to fight for your marriage. Most people refuse to forgive; but every effort must be made for reconciliation.

Many people try to work it out on their own and fail to do so, so they need to find mature spiritual counselors. Sex therapy doesn't work—it only complicates the matter.

The next thing one has to do is to evaluate all the persons within their scope of influence to see if those persons are adding to or subtracting from their marriage.

Great effort must always be made to improve communication with each other and stay away from anything that promotes immorality so that no unnecessary doors are open to healthy relationships.

Husbands and wives must forgive. If an act of infidelity took place in the past and resulted in a child being born outside the marriage, then work together to include the child or your spouse. There must be boundaries. The parent of that child ought not to go visiting the child alone—more will result.

The Stress of Breaking Up

Breaking up at any time is not something that is easy to do or to deal with—whether the relationship is political, familial, contractual, or any other kind!

I believe that we are in a season where there will be quite a few breakups and break-offs! Some we can avoid, and some we cannot; but the key thing to remember is when separation takes place, close all doors gently.

I don't support or condone the slander, character defamation, violent fights, and even killings when relationships end—whether the relationships are political or between spouses! Don't let it be that all along, throughout the relationship, you didn't find faults until the relationship ended, and then is when you begin to tell the world how "bad" the person was and proceed to throw stones at what you are leaving behind!

We find that as persons leave an organization, business, or church, those who leave proceed to curse, defame, or slander the leaders and organizations they leave behind! Oftentimes, the fault does not lie with who is left behind but with those who leave!

King David was always wary of those who would leave and speak negatively about the leaders they left behind; he never embraced them because he knew that it would not be long before their true colors were revealed and they would do the same to him in no time.

The Breaking

Over the years, we have seen a number of murders take place as a result of breakups. We need to look into every relationship and see the foundation on which it started and see if it is God's will! How "good" sex is or how deeply you may fall in love with a person is not what determines whether or not the relationship is what God wants for you! In counseling many over the years, there is a central theme that runs through many of these relationships—they say if they can't have the person, then no one else can have them, so they will either kill them or resort to witchcraft! Some say the thought of someone else having sex with their partner, if the partner left them, enrages them.

FAMILY, THE FIRST LINE OF GOVERNMENT

Before a person gets into a relationship, the first relationship he/she needs to have is a relationship with God—who will ultimately direct him/her to make right choices. In understanding true love, you must first love God and then love yourself! Even Christians make the mistake of becoming unequally yoked by entering relationships they ought not to. Being unequally yoked is as if an ox and a donkey come together to plow a field (Deuteronomy 22:10). These two animals cannot work together because their views/ goals/objectives/approach to deal with the task are different! One may want to go to church or to engage in living holy, while the other person does not want that; nor do they want their partner to engage in that; and they want to party all the time, or may be extremely possessive, or have more than one person (or a spouse) while trying to control the other person.

There are many third parties who desperately want to break off the relationships—especially after finding out that their partner either is married or has someone else—but because of the power and influence that the person they are with commands, they are fearful for their lives. In fact, sometimes when they go to the police station to report any abuse, they end up having to "deal with" the policemen, too, in return for protection!

Lack of communication is also a huge factor in breakups! Sometimes prosperity, academic elevation, and upward mobility of any kind often cause change in a person's sphere of influence. Such a person may feel the need to elevate himself/herself socially. So old friends go, and they embrace a different class of people. They don't remember where they are coming from and the hardships they have been through with their spouse/partner. God allows us to go through hardships, to prepare us and to set a foundation for the blessings He has ahead for us, so that when the blessings do come, they will not destroy us!

Dealing with breakups is not easy—this is why it is important for each of us to have a strong relationship with God first and foremost. You then need to have Godly, objective people around us so they can encourage you in the right direction, give you sound Godly advice, and pray for strength or the grace to go through!

CHAPTER 25

ORDER IN THE CHURCH: SEXUAL IMPURITY

The cry locally and globally regarding sexual impurity in the church on the part of the church leader begs a very important question and provides an opportunity for correcting and teaching: Were those with the titles of Bishop or Pastor within the local church afraid to address these serious matters because they were afraid of financial fallout and popularity? Everyone needs to really read and seek to understand 1 Corinthians 5. We need to judge within the church and let God deal with the world.

The Church seriously needs to look at how they select leaders—are they selected by level of education and societal status? Leaders must be selected by the Holy Spirit and the Word, particularly Acts 6, 1 Timothy 3:6, and Luke 6:12–17.

Is the church putting young converts and people—those who are untested—who are consumed with pride in positions of leadership in the Church (1 Timothy 3:6)? These days, people turn into Bishops and Apostles overnight and have quite a large following thereafter without them being tested or proven.

When a leader of a church—whether Pastor, Bishop, or Prophet—commits sexual sins openly, and it is exposed, they are still kept in the position without correction or restoration, and then they call it grace! (Galatians 6:1). Part of the restoration process includes discipline; for example, putting them to sit down for a year while they receive counseling.

If the Church supports common-law relationships or marries those who are unequally yoked according to the scriptures (2 Corinthians 6), then it means the church is also upholding sexual impurity and opens the door for such.

What about worship teams and musicians? They are now operating like stars, and many of them are walking in sexual impurity when they are supposed to be the most holy ministry in the Church. Yet we allow them to operate, and that opens the door to sexual immorality and defilement of the congregations. (Read *In His Presence* by Pastor Michelle Lyston.) They mix with the world and think God is OK with it. So because we no longer allow the Holy Spirit, the Word of God, and Jesus Christ to be the Center, the Body of Christ is now paying the price. If one belief is not lining up with the Word of God, then we are not even supposed to listen to them (read Galatians 1:8).

Finally, many people attend churches, but did God lead them to where they are going, or is it simply a physical attraction?

Immorality Defiles the Church

Every generation must have a Samuel; otherwise, the Church will be set back immeasurably. If there is not a strong spiritual leader, the people will perish. The main fact that the Philistines are not afraid to attack or march against the Church, it is a clear indication of the sin that exists within. The scripture 1 Samuel 7:3–4 says: "Then Samuel spoke to all the house of Israel, saying, 'If you return to the LORD with all your hearts, *then* put away the foreign Gods and the Ashtoreths from among you, and prepare your hearts for the LORD, and serve Him only; and He will deliver you from the hand of the Philistines.' So the children of Israel put away the Baals and the Ashtoreths, and served the LORD only."

It must be duly noted that the Philistine was a domestic and not a foreign enemy. The *Philistine* illustrates the power of the enemy inside the professing Christian Church and is more to be dreaded than any enemy who stands outside.

Immorality is now dominating the world. Many are celebrating worldwide, while others are asking the question, "Where is God in all this?"

But before the church leaders can deal with the varying issues successfully and win the battle against immorality, they will need to admit their shortcomings, fall on their faces, and repent before the Lord. They cannot try to use the ark as a magic symbol, thinking it will atone for their evildoings and guarantee the presence and blessing of God.

Immorality in the Church

Paul, the Apostle, makes clear the seriousness of the level of immorality in the Church. Immorality was considered so serious that Paul says we must withdraw ourselves from them and not even eat from them. He was referring to immoral people in the Church who claimed to be Christians. The Church has been compromising for years with immoral Christians, and now we are reaping the rewards of that.

If the Church wants to see change in the world with regard to immorality, then the time has come to administer strict discipline when Christians openly persist in sin and do not heed corrective counsel.

Leave the world to God, and let God judge the world. Very shortly, many of them will be crying—weeping—for what they have done.

We need to stop transferring the compromising Pastors, Priests, musicians, singers, and officers of the local churches that are involved in immorality and are still serving in the local church, and put them out if they fail to be restored!

Immorality is not only a sin against the body but also against the Holy Spirit! (1 Corinthians 6:9–10; 2 Corinthians 5:9–13).

To deal with immorality in the Church, the Church will need to engage in the very things that it has been resisting—the ministry of Deliverance (Mark 1, 5). Perversion is an unclean spirit that perverts the course of justice, destroys families, brings people into error, and twists, coils, and distorts the Biblical doctrine. Anyone who professes to be a Christian who also supports or justifies immorality within or outside the Church is walking in error and is being influenced by the spirit of perversion.

Immorality cannot be defeated through the flesh or the legal system. It is defeated by the spirit of grace and supplication (Ephesians 4:18). The issues of abortion, gambling, child abuse, pornography, atheism, filthy minds, and doctrinal error all work in conjunction with immorality. Additionally, the love of money and whoredoms are all connected to immorality.

It attacks and defiles spiritual leaders, judges, lawyers, lawmakers, high-ranking officials, and people poised for greatness.

Sex is a gift of God, and from that perspective, it allows one to imitate God's image; thus, all improper sexual activity is seen as an affront to God and the lowering of human dignity.

The Church is now in a great era to reestablish the Deliverance ministry and the Spiritual Gifts. It is time to begin administering serious discipline for those within the House and feed and help those who are on the streets and are caught up in immorality; show them the love of Jesus and bring them back to the fold.

We need to teach members of the Church how to conduct themselves in the various environments and the importance of waiting and seeking the Lord on whom He has chosen for them. The Church has to win the battle within before they can deal with the battle on the outside, or else they will fall before the Philistines (1 Samuel 4:10).

CHAPTER 26

SEXUAL IMPURITY DEFILES A NATION

S exual impurity and the love of money are eating away at the society. People are using their wealth to pervert the society. Media groups and Human Rights groups and organizations that were started to help humanity have become caught up in that web, and they are pushing it—sadly, many young lives are being destroyed as a result!

If sex is such a private issue, then why is that "private" issue being promoted so publicly? Why are all the antics and happenings that take place in that private zone being distorted and pushed into the public arena?

When did sex become more important than the humanitarian cause to save a life or a soul?

The Role of an NGO

The role of a Non-Governmental Organization (NGO) is to promote social values, local initiatives, problem-solving, poverty eradication, and cultural and health education to empower the masses. Promoting and executing justice, bringing change especially to grassroots people, are also part of the process. Every NGO must operate in truth and integrity. NGOs should, in no case, use funds to corrupt or destroy lives.

The recent happenings in Jamaica regarding certain sexually-driven materials to sensitize youth and adults alike on oral and anal sex is not just happening in Jamaica to the less fortunate and the less privileged but is happening throughout the globe. Many people's lives are being destroyed by it.

The role of government is to protect the poor and the needy at any cost—especially the children. Government in no way should compromise—regardless of the loans and grants they receive from the varying entities.

I have always said that the people of the nation should be made knowledgeable of the terms of every grant or loan the nation is receiving and what it is all tied to. Some things that people think are blessings are in fact curses! Similarly, voters within a nation need to examine their representatives to see what they really believe in, and the media should ensure that it is clear during their campaigns what they believe. People need to stop selecting people based on money or popularity. People should make their selections based on the individual's strong morals, social values, and attitudes—must be the number-one criteria!

The Defilement of a Nation

The Bible clearly speaks about the fact that sexual impurity can defile a nation. Oral and anal sex, adultery, and fornication defile and destroy any nation. King David's sexual problem—when he committed adultery with Bathsheba—defiled and destroyed the entire foundation of his administration, which opened the door for other issues to plague the nation, and it significantly affected his family by way of his children (2 Samuel 13:1–21).

It is going to take the effort of every person within the nation to deal with this unclean spirit of perversion that is destroying the nation. Every person has to look into him/her self and ask the question, *Am I walking in sexual purity?* If you are any position of authority or leadership of any kind—church, civic, political, business—you are opening the door for the plagues to plunder the vulnerable. It is important to note that a plague is referring not only to a disease or poor physical health but also to other things that continually and significantly affect us. So increases in murders, rapes, economic failures, continued debt, poverty, and other woes on the nation would be regarded as plagues! Laws may change. Times may change. Worldviews may change. But God's Word does not change on the issue of sexual impurity! (Matthew 24:35).

Recognize that sex is more than a physical act; it is also spiritual. When two people engage in sex, their souls also become knitted together; an agreement—covenant—takes place, and the two become one flesh! The scripture 1 Corinthians 6:16 says, "Or do you not know that he who is joined to a harlot is one body *with her?* For 'the two,' He says, 'shall become one flesh.'"

You do the math. If a man or woman sleeps with five persons for the week, with how many persons has his/her soul been knitted? Furthermore, when a soul is knitted, it is not undone overnight, because it was not meant to happen that way. The only person that can deliver that man or woman is Jesus.

Now, suppose you are the head of an organization and you sleep with a harlot. You become a harlot as well! So, then, a harlot is the head of the organization.

A word to the wealthy: riches are of transient value. You must be good stewards of your earthly wealth. Earthly riches are only as good as the present value, and what you do with your wealth is an investment with eternal rewards. Be careful of how you invest. Remember, too, that what is valuable today may become worthless tomorrow.

The Rising of the Spirit of Incest

The year 2017 is a very significant year for every believer to rise up and fulfill their God-given purpose. We must walk in obedience, according to Deuteronomy 28:1–14, to receive the promise. Many persons have great expectations, but those will only come to fruition if we begin to change some things about ourselves now. We have to

- renew our minds daily;
- let our light shine;
- seek God daily; and
- obey the instructions of the Lord.

Prophetic Revelation

The Lord is showing me that the spirit of incest will rise—fathers will want to have sex with their daughters and uncles with their nieces. It is happening right across the board with families to destroy the institution of family, and many are afraid to talk. We need to rise up against this spirit that is rising up to destroy the family. We also need to deal with the spirit of incest, which is also destroying the church. Pastors and Bishops are "feasting" on the flock, and many of the churches sweep it under the carpet while they allow them to remain on the pulpit. But they must remember 1 Timothy 3. God is going to expose more of these issues. If we are the church and we are supposed to bring healing to the world, then it must start within the church. The spirit of Eli has to be broken, and *holiness* must reign if we are going to deal effectively with perversion and the spirit of incest.

We also need to cry out against the media and Hollywood, who are promoting perversion and incest. It is extremely rampant, especially among Caucasians. Pray for Maryland. Pray against riots in Indianapolis. Pray for the state of Alaska, as government officials are planning to go there regarding oil-potential problems. Pray for the souls of Beyoncé, Kim Kardashian, Lady Gaga, Jamaican singer Sanchez, and Boy George. Pray also against a freak accident on Usain Bolt. He needs to seek the Lord and turn his life over to the Lord now. Single Christians need to read the story of Ruth in the Bible again and line up accordingly. Pray against meteorites creating havoc and against severe cosmic activities. Donald Trump needs to be wise regarding Russia. Russia is not his friend. There is a subtle plan to trap him, and it can cause impeachment and topple his presidency. He needs to seek God as never before. The enemy will not come in a way to which he is accustomed. They are coming in suits and ties.

Break the Cycle of Sexual Addiction

Sexual addiction is eating away the society and the nations! It negatively affects the economy and propels wrong choices and poor decisions. Sexual addiction can be so strong that it can even cause wars to begin.

Sexual addiction comes as a result of/through the "doors" of adultery, fornication, incest, masturbation, homosexuality, lesbianism, sadomasochism, pedophilia, lust, phone/Internet sex, use of artificial instruments, and doctrinal error.

Sexual perversion cannot be dealt with by legislation or therapy. Perversion is a stronghold that starts oftentimes from the mother's womb (Psalm 51:5, 2 Corinthians 10). Strongholds pass from one generation to the next when it has not been addressed.

This stronghold attacks those who are destined for greatness. Its mandate is to terminate their God-given purpose. Most that are trapped in perversion will tell you that they want to do good—but they are trapped, and because sex is such a private issue, most are afraid to discuss their struggle or confide in someone. Even in marriages, they are afraid to discuss it with their partner. It affects their marriage and turns them off completely from sex.

Dealing with the Root

To deal with perversion, we must deal with the root cause. The root often stems from childhood. Sometimes just playing "house/dolly-house" or "cousin and cousin boil good soup" opens the door for sexual perversion to enter. A child who has been raped, has been a victim of incest, has been fondled, or was born outside of wedlock, as well as persons who have had abortions, all have this stronghold.

What explanation do we give to a child who has "wet dreams" or who dreams that they are having sex with someone? These are signs that there is perversion within the family line.

Strongholds can also be transferred, and sex is a method of transference. Sex joins souls to each other and is a binding agreement (soul tie). So when one loses his/her virginity, a binding agreement takes place, and if it occurs out of wedlock and there is a separation (breakup) and then marriage takes place to someone else, then there is trouble in the marriage. Many married couples today will tell you that they cannot get "turned on" unless they watch some kind of pornography or sexually explicit scenes.

When one lies with a harlot/prostitute or several sex partners, one also becomes one flesh with the persons one sleeps (1 Corinthians 6:16).

To be free from sexual addiction, one must admit the problem and that it is wrong. They have to walk away from anything that seems perverted. Remember, sex is a covenant! It is more than a physical experience! It involves a communion of lives, and since Christ is one with the believer's spirit, it is unthinkable to be involved in immorality.

Sexual intercourse involves our whole being. It has far-reaching effect with great spiritual significance and social complications. Sexual behavior involves self-identity. When an individual is involved in this sin, they sin against their bodies (1 Corinthians 6:18), and it leaves the individual open to diseases. Some people may be going to the gym to get healthy; but if they do that while engaged in sexual addiction, then they are defeating the purpose.

What to do to be Free

- You must admit that it is wrong and walk away from it.
- You must be disciplined. Deliverance is a process. They must keep away from the old places and old lovers, stop texting and calling, and keep away from websites and social networks that foster or encourage sexual perversion. Remember, it is a yoke, and yokes can be destroyed by going into God's presence or speaking with a genuine deliverance minister.

- Be open with your partner and tell him/her what you have been through. Pray together and agree in prayer.
- Have daily communion at home and renounce and confess your sins before God.
- Forgive! Forgive those who have raped or abused you. Bless those that curse you.
- Stay away from groups that are involved in perversion, even if they are Christians or are close to you (1 Corinthians 5:11).
- Be careful who lies in your marital bed!
- Don't engage in threesomes and orgies.
- Where you have been molested by family members, tell it to your parents (if they are alive), even if you are now an adult!
- Confess Psalm 51 and declare Psalm 91 daily.

Pray for the Sexual Purity of Your Leaders

As we are all seeing these days, there are many sexual scandals taking place locally and globally among leaders in general, and even churchmen. However, this should be no surprise, because strong leaders come under great temptation on a daily basis. Furthermore, people are generally attracted to power of any kind at any level. Strong leaders also struggle with sexual impurity. David in the Bible, for example, struggled with lust. We are in an era where there are no more "ugly" people because you can buy anything to "enhance" what you have or cover up what you don't. People can now purchase lashes, eye color, breasts, and bottoms, and you can even change your complexion if you wish.

There is a war going on to bring down strong leaders in the society across the board. It doesn't just include churchmen but also doctors, lawyers, teachers, politicians, and businessmen. In fact, even a strong group leader in an unknown group is a target. Because what this will do is bring the family to the point of instability and bring more hate, more bitterness, and a greater divide from the family level to the national level.

There should be no rejoicing when a church leader, or any other leader for that matter, falls. The scripture 1 Peter 4:17 says, "For the time has come for judgment to begin at the house of God; and if it begins with us first, what will be the end of those who do not obey the gospel of God?" If the Lord allows this for those within the church, can you imagine what lies ahead for the rest of the world? Put on your seat belts and get ready for this ride!

God is now ready to deal with sexual impurity, which is now eating away at the moral fabric of society. Don't hide some and expose others with great outcry. That will not augur well for anyone.

Strong Leaders

Strong leaders need to have strong protocol to which they need to adhere resolutely. They need to surround themselves with strong support. For example, leaders need to have their wives/husbands upfront with them at all times. Even within the church, sometimes the wives are left out and given a seat at the back. Unfortunately, it is a common culture within the church generally—the culture of "women must keep silent." They will shower the men with a lot of attention and things, but the men ignore the wives completely if it is the husband who is the leader. The opposite is also true. Recognize that it is both of them who are called, not just the husband *or* wife. This happens among all facets: politics, business, legal fraternity, etc. You should not have a bodyguard, chauffeur, gardener, or armor-bearer of the opposite gender moving around alone with your spouse. All of these can lead to sexual impurity, and it is real! Bodyguards will take the "body," the chauffeur will drive away with your family, the gardener will till and tend to the soil, the helper will help herself to your spouse, and the armor-bearer will disarm you. Even companies and governments are sending away their employees with members of the opposite gender on business trips for extended periods to five-star hotels—without their families. Their families ought to be included, or those employees will certainly see stars!

Opportunity

Out of crises, there are always great opportunities:

- Church people must pray for the sexual purity and satisfaction of leaders across the board. Too much time is spent praying for money and other things, ignoring the reality of the struggle they face. They must pray that the eyes of the leaders remain consecrated and will not focus on anybody else other than their own spouse. They must also pray that those leaders who are not married remain steady and focused until they have one.
- Why should someone need a personal trainer? Why should there be the need for lap dancing to be taught? Recognize that when the focus and attention are placed on the physical, that is exactly where the devil wants our focus, and that is where the door opens for sexual impurity to flood in. That aspect is the most private and personal area of our lives.
- Leaders need to be careful when they are counseling persons of the opposite gender by themselves—especially church leaders!
- Parents need to teach their children about sexual purity and how they ought to dress. This means that parents need to lead by example.
- If the media is going to be any kind of watchdog, then they are also going to need to cut down on the profanity, looseness, and immorality to which they expose our children and youth.
- The church, overall, needs to embrace the Deliverance Ministry as in the book of Acts.

CHAPTER 27

GUARD YOUR HEART! GOD WANTS INTIMACY!

The heart is the source of all evil actions. It is not what we eat that defiles us; it is what we say. Our heart must always align with our lips having good things. True worship requires that the heart and mouth be aligned together (Matthew 15:7–9). In the same way, praise and true worship must come from the depth of our hearts.

There are many things we need to guard on a daily basis to be consecrated—our heart, ears, eyes, and mouth. That is why, as Christians, we must be careful to what and to whom we listen on a daily basis. Gossip and negative conversations can bring defilement and allow a person to lose his/her blessings.

God is calling His people in this season into the deep!

There are many things found in the *deep*! There are many mysteries hidden within the deep. He is calling us into a place where we can discern our environment, where we will be able to discern the clean from the unclean and the holy from the unholy.

He wants us to know the plans He has for each of us, hence He is calling us into His Secret Place (Psalm 91).

Many are seeking the things of the world while they ignore the things of God that will bring them into spiritual bankruptcy. There is a release taking place in this season, and only in the secret place will that release happen. It is critical that oil remains in your lamp! (Matthew 25). Right now, there are many mysteries and blessings passing by. Psalm 42:1–2 says, "As the deer pants for the water brooks, so pants my soul for You, O God. My soul thirsts for God, for the living God. When shall I come and appear before God?"

The water represents the Holy Spirit. Water is also used naturally for refreshing. Furthermore, in the natural, when a predator tries to catch a deer, it runs to the water for protection. As a result, their scent becomes undetectable. So when the deer run into the water, not only are they hidden but also they are refreshed! Likewise, when we run to the Holy Spirit and hide in Him, we are hidden—the enemy cannot track or discern us—meanwhile, we are being refreshed by the Holy Spirit!

Christians Must Discern

In light of all the deception that is taking place worldwide and within the Church, it is critical for Christians to do as the scriptures admonishes and discern.

We need to recognize that we are being sensitized through numerous media tools—advertising, movies, songs, and jingles. There is a constant twisting and play on words as well as blatant changes in the use and meanings of words. There are many who take words that are positive, even the Word of God, and taint them by twisting them and turning them into something impure and negative.

Christians ought not to hold independent views on anything; as followers of Christ, a Christian's view must be based on the written Word of God. The Word of God is the only true light that can dispel spiritual darkness. It is the eternal logos and the only true light; everything was created by the Word—through Him, by Him, and for Him! (John 1:3). Nothing changes without the Word. If the Bible is useless, why is there so much fight to get rid of it?

There is no scriptural reference that God created secular or civil society. The only thing God separated was light from darkness. Romans 13:1 reminds us: "Let every soul be subject to the governing authorities. For there is no authority except from God, and the authorities that exist are appointed by God."

Both secular and spiritual leadership and authority were instituted by God and must never to be used for personal gain or to control or dominate others. Every leader is accountable to God (Daniel 4:32; Psalm 75:6–7). God does not sanction unjust legislation. He will allow evil rulers at times, as is exemplified through Nebuchadnezzar and Pharaoh, to get His people back in line. God grants authority to serve good end. How the authority is exercised will be brought into accountability regarding those to whom authority has been given.

Battle of Doctrines

Every Christian must know that it is critical for him/her. Behind every doctrine is a spirit. If the doctrine is true, then the Holy Spirit is behind it. If the doctrine is false, then God is not in it. As believers, we must know what God sanctions. Everything that is in conflict with the Word of God is not of God. Likewise, anyone that denies the existence of Christ is the spirit of the Antichrist.

Behind every spirit, there is a lie, and behind every lie, there is bondage. Lies are strongholds and place personal bondage where God's Word has been subjugated. To every non-scriptural idea or personally confessed belief that is held to be true and behind every lie, there are idols. Idols are established where there exists a failure to trust in the provision of God and His principles to transform nations and bring peace.

It is critical for Christians to be careful what sounds they listen to. You have to understand that whoever dominates the airwaves has a greater control of the environment, and this is why Christians must think and speak positively. They must be bold in declaring, naming, and renaming some things. One of the things Christians have been doing is keeping away from the political arena on the basis of a false doctrine.

Christians need to utilize their spiritual and financial resources as well as their votes! They must also employ the fervent use of prayer.

Fruit of the Spirit

Christians need to test the spirits within and without! There is too much deception, and many Christians are falling away in the midst of it all. It is interesting that the Church is the first place certain people run to when they need mass endorsement. It is even more interesting that they can't or won't speak against certain rights groups, fraternal, civic organizations, and even other religions, but they have no hesitation coming against Christianity with great intensity.

Many Christians are ashamed to quote Bible verses. However, Christians must use the Word to test the authenticity of anything presented to them. Some are even ashamed to be called Pastor; they prefer to be addressed as doctor. So now those have found themselves lost in the middle of arguments on worldview and in the position of compromise.

Christians must be able to discern true from false prophets/teachers. A false prophet is not one who gives a word that does not come to pass. It is one who presents the way of salvation or of sanctification as other than the cross (2 Peter 2). They engage in subtle reasoning, heresy, science, evolution, and philosophical views, and twist scriptures and words, moving people from the path. They exploit instead of developing.

Christians, *do not* be caught unawares or be oblivious! Discern the truth and recognize that the enemy is more dangerous within than without!

CHAPTER 28

LOVE: THE MOST MISQUOTED, MISUSED, AND MISUNDERSTOOD WORD

Hebrews 12:6–11 says, "For whom the Lord loves He chastens, and scourges every son whom He receives. If you endure chastening, God deals with you as with sons; for what son is there whom a father does not chasten? But if you are without chastening, of which all have become partakers, then you are illegitimate and not sons. Furthermore, we have had human fathers who corrected us, and we paid them respect. Shall we not much more readily be in subjection to the Father of spirits and live? For they indeed for a few days chastened us as seemed best to them, but He for our profit, that we may be partakers of His holiness. Now no chastening seems to be joyful for the present, but painful; nevertheless, afterward it yields the peaceable fruit of righteousness to those who have been trained by it."

Many times I have listened to secular social, moral, and ethical debates on the issue of love, and many times people misunderstand the true context of what love really is. Ninety percent of the deception that reaches people comes through the use of this very word. John 3:16

clearly states what true love is. Which politician or lobby group has ever given his/her life for another to have life? Furthermore, 1 Corinthians 13 speaks about sixteen characteristics of love—regardless of who we are and what we do. If we are not measured with those characteristics of love, regardless of our profession, occupation, or whatever we do for others, if it is not motivated by love, then it doesn't make sense. It is love alone that makes us like God (1 John 4:7). Many times, even within the Church, when people are corrected and told the truth, they say there is no love. That is not so! It *is* in fact love! Anyone who refuses correction or chastening by the Heavenly Father, spiritual parents, and biological parents are—by Biblical Standards—illegitimate. Likewise, anyone who refuses to speak Biblical truth on a situation is not operating in love! Anyone who compromises the truth and condones it is operating in deception and not love.

Many times people will try to make Jesus a part of the deception of true love. God loves people—it is why He gave up His only Son to die for people. But when one rejects the love and sacrifice Jesus made, how then can we talk about love? Just think of your father dying and giving his life so you can receive an inheritance, and all you want is the inheritance; you don't honor, respect, appreciate, or thank your father—is that love?

Many say they love God, but love is an action word, and so many refuse to honor him! Meanwhile, they will say they love family members, children, and other loved ones, and then cheer them on when they are doing wrong—and say that is love! That is *not* love; that is hypocrisy!

People have become lovers of themselves! Politicians pass laws for our children to smoke marijuana, carry out abortions, and other immoralities, while so many are on the streets homeless, hungry, sick, and suffering. Pastors refuse to tell their people the truth to have church growth and large bank accounts!

Recognize that Jesus never condoned sin, and, oftentimes, people try to connect the name of the Lord with sin and try to justify it by saying God is a God of love. Jesus died for our sins and resurrected and ascended so that we may take advantage of the opportunity to walk away from sin and embrace a life of hope and trust in Him to help us overcome sin. He loves us, but He hates our sins!

The basis on which everything must be built or done is love! Many say they keep/observe the Ten Commandments, but when money becomes a person's idol, he/she is already breaking at least one commandment! Remember the rich young ruler who would not give up his riches to serve the Lord? Money was already his idol.

While praying recently, the Lord revealed that He is about to get the attention of the rich! We are about to see fire and floods globally as never before, especially with prominent buildings. He is about to promote the nations that have shown love by standing up for righteousness and truth! He is also ready to show love to many Pastors that have walked away because of the riches of the world. He is calling them back now because He needs them.

Show true love today and touch someone's heart! Not in word but in deed!

Deception

Whether it be religion, politics, marketing strategy, or scientific theory, every belief must be validated by (1) the Bible and (2) the law of the land. People, whether religious or nonreligious, are quicker to believe scientific theories of evolution without even the scientific fact behind it. Scientific facts are Biblically supported, but scientific theories are not and are, in fact, conflicting the facts. I did not evolve from fish or monkey! The Bible is the inspired Word of God recorded through God's holy apostles and prophets. People prefer to accept the theories of Einstein, who was also a man. With that said, 80 percent of the people don't read their Bibles. Only those who don't read the Bible could be deceived, particularly concerning the post above. There will be many anti-Christ individuals and groups. The word *anti* means "against." However, there is *the* Antichrist that has not yet been revealed. As you must already be aware, for every major event, there is always an advent. There will be many who will say they are the Christ—the Bible tells us so. Matthew 24:5 says, "For many will come in My name, saying, 'I am the Christ,' and will deceive many." (Read also Matthew 24:22–25.) Furthermore, when a man does not believe in Christ or in the Bible, that in itself is also a religion. If you believe in your own self, that is a religion too!

The people involved in such groups clearly did not read the Bible for themselves; nor did they seek the Lord for a revelation of His Word, which is one of the benefits of serving the Lord; the capacity to speak freely with Him and receive from Him directly.

The Bible says in Matthew 7:15–23, "Beware of false prophets, who come to you in sheep's clothing, but inwardly they are ravenous wolves. You will know them by their fruits. Do men gather grapes from thornbushes or figs from thistles? Even so, every good tree bears good fruit, but a bad tree bears bad fruit. A good tree cannot bear bad fruit, nor can a bad tree bear good fruit. Every tree that does not bear good fruit is cut down and thrown into the fire. Therefore by their fruits you will know them. Not everyone who says to Me, 'Lord, Lord,' shall enter the kingdom of heaven, but he who does the will of My Father in heaven. Many will say to Me in that day, 'Lord, Lord, have we not prophesied in Your name, cast out demons in Your name, and done many wonders in Your name?' And then I will declare to them, 'I never knew you; depart from Me, you who practice lawlessness!'"

The scripture 1 John 4:1 reminds us: "Beloved, do not believe every spirit, but test the spirits, whether they are of God; because many false prophets have gone out into the world." And the only way you can test the spirit is to use the Biblical guidelines/measuring stick. The books of 1 John, Peter, Thessalonians, Ephesians, and so on tell us all about the works of the devil.

Why is it that each time people get tricked by the devil because they refuse to surrender to God and to read His Word and instead blame God? I bet if a true prophet went proclaiming the truth, they would not follow him! Why is it that a woman, for example, will get deceived by a "fake" man and the false emotions and fake expressions of "love," but when the real one comes, she doesn't accept or embrace him?

Many people are drawn to hype, pretty speeches, and everything they see, because they believe they have all that is required to make a true evaluation on their own. People always value people by the face/surface, but they don't know the heart. Everything starts in the heart.

The Antichrist will be an excellent actor, orator, dresser, or liar, and his appearance will be flawless, and that is what people tend to go for generally. It is the same reason people will flock to the huge church building with the stained glass windows and ten choirs and all the other physical amenities but will not enter the doors of a small sanctuary with louver windows.

People are looking for God in the midst of extravagance, when He chooses to enter by way of humble surroundings! Thus—*the Manger*! There are many bad products that come in excellent packaging and flamboyant marketing strategies, and people love it! Thus, the deception!

Who Is the Real Boss?

Every boss or leader from every sector needs to take time out to evaluate him/herself, his/her organization, and all the people they supervise. Oftentimes, leaders and bosses fail to recognize the real value within their organization. The lack of willingness to change is hindered by a seducing spirit. A seducing spirit influences persons to undermine and usurp by beguiling, flirting, provoking, and deceiving. It is attracted to weak leaders and those who are destined for greatness. This spirit attacks both males and females. It negatively affects or influences decision-making. Persons being used by this spirit should know that it feeds on their doubt and limits their vision.

Many of the mistakes that we have made in the society are influenced by the seducing spirit. Every boss or leader needs to know that once you are entrusted with power and authority, his/her daily decision-making must be fair and justified without any negative influence.

Both increase and decrease come through association. It is critical for you to have the right team and inner circle around you for growth and success. The right team is not necessarily made up of persons that will tell you what you want to hear all the time. If someone tells you what you want to hear all the time or is there to stroke your ego (2 Chronicles 18; Luke 6:26), then you are being set up for a fall.

This sort of setup is made up of persons who behave as if they are the best workers in the organization. They let the boss know all the personal sacrifices they have made for the organization—especially for the boss—and lets the boss believe that they have his/her back. They will even get the boss or leader to confide in them, share secrets with them, and feel obligated to them. They then use this information as a bargaining tool against the boss/leader for promotion and personal gain.

Think About This . . .

Have you ever been close to making a business deal or to seizing a huge opportunity, and then, suddenly, everything falls apart and goes down the drain? Then you were hindered by a seducing spirit.

Have you ever been in the position where you know you have been genuinely faithful, and, suddenly, the boss or leader has turned against you or you turn against the boss? Then a seducing spirit was the reason.

Have you ever been next in line for promotion, and, suddenly, everything is cancelled and you hear that the board members changed their minds? The seducing spirit was in operation.

People who operate under this spirit divert leadership from the path of righteousness. These people love office gossip. They hinder production and productivity. They love gift-giving and flirting also, but at the end of the day, their assignment is to take you out and take over. They are loyal to no one. Sometimes, it is the person you least expect!

These kinds of people turn off new investment and new opportunities, and sometimes they block those that God would send to help the organization. They also hinder the right persons from getting promoted and bring down great leaders.

Sadly, this kind of person/personality is not limited to organizations but can wreak havoc on families. It can be a family member, close friend, gardener, secretary—anyone! Look carefully and without prejudice! Sometimes whom you think is your friend is your enemy and whom you may think is your enemy is actually your friend.

Effective Leadership

To be effective, you must remember that the first thing God did in Creation was to separate light from darkness. God is the epitome of light! For a new day, we must begin to walk in true Light.

Bosses and leaders need to examine their decisions for the past three years. "Who influenced your decisions?" "How can you make amends if your decision-making was wrongly influenced?" "Were my actions justified?" "Have the decisions that I have made seem fair, or did they seem to be influenced?" "Do I pray before acting on something that comes to my attention and I need to make a decision?" "Is everyone in the organization getting a fair opportunity to excel?" "Am I bold enough to take a stand in the organization, regardless of the outcome, for expansion and growth?" "Who is the real boss?"

CHAPTER 29

HEALTHY MIND, HEALTHY LIVING

Philippians 4:8 reminds us: "Finally, brethren, whatever things are true, whatever things are noble, whatever things are just, whatever things are pure, whatever things are lovely, whatever things are of good report, if there is any virtue and if there is anything praiseworthy—meditate on these things."

There are so many things that come against our minds on a daily basis to hinder us from remaining pure, positive, and prosperous. The battles always begin in our minds. We have to mentally fight false doctrines, lies, demonic views, strongholds, fear, and even idols that have been established within the mind.

Our minds determine our feelings, affect our health, gather information, and decide what to believe as a result of repetition. A person cannot improve his/her mental capabilities until he/she has a pure and healthy mind. It is therefore critical for us to renew our minds on a daily basis, and that can only come about through prayer and meditating on God's Word. Many of us have been taught some negative things over the years that we thought were true and became the norm. But the onus would now be on us to identify and keep the truth. Joshua 1:8 reminds us: "This Book of the Law shall not depart from your mouth, but you shall meditate in it day and night that you may observe to do according to all that is written in it. For then you will make your way prosperous, and then you will have good success."

Surprisingly, a story recently published in *The Gleaner* of a high school that carries the name of the Trinity was bragging of the success of new age philosophy they embraced and implemented. It is not just that they were employing a program but that the very root of the principles employed goes against the Word that they stand on as a Church-based school. The after effects on those young minds in the long run will be detrimental and may even require "exorcism."

In the same way, we cannot win a war against poverty unless the transformation takes place within the mind. A garrison is a state of the mind. If you move persons from a garrison out of that area and put them in a different (nongarrison) area, they will still function in the same way, unless the mind is renewed. This is why they can use trained people to divide them all the time, because all you need is a trained writer, an excellent psychologist, and a good orator or university professor with the same way of thinking.

A mind that is not renewed is unable to discern right from wrong, good from bad, or identify the perfect will of God—not for themselves or for the nation. Our nation has been out of God's will for many years, but we still think we are OK. While the lives of the people become worse, others benefit from that.

A polluted mind becomes blind and is pulled away by every wind of doctrine. Some of the things that seem normal become life threatening for other people. Sadly, we have allowed some of the Hollywood stars and music moguls to pollute our minds and the minds of our children. Even the video games have played their roles in polluting the minds of our future leaders. There are some deep things that have been embedded in our culture that are rooted in witchcraft, but we have been convinced that, regardless of that fact, we are not to let those things go and that to reject it is to reject a part of ourselves. Not so. We *must* necessarily let go of those things that are not God's will for us or instructions to us.

A Healthy Mind

God wants us to have a healthy mind—one of power, love, and soundness. Fear is one of the biggest hindrances to us and to our nation. We don't even know who we truly are and in what or whom we believe. We must value and protect our mind, emotions, and will.

We must recognize that people in our nation have reached a boiling point because of the lies, false doctrines, injustices, and manipulation, and it is only a matter of time before everything boils over into pockets of civil disturbances. We can't continue to pass laws, blame the police, and not recognize that if the root is not addressed in the right way, then we are in for an implosion. The mind can be either a powerful tool for positive change or a weapon of destruction. People don't even care anymore what is being spewed out over the airwaves. Morals have broken down, so minds have been defiled and impure. Remember that whatever we think about and meditate on is what we act out (Proverbs 23:7; Romans 7:23).

Hurting People Hurt People

It is critical to screen people before they are established in influential positions. We have to look beyond just academic qualifications. There needs to be spiritual and psychological evaluations carried out.

It is important to deal with any traumatic happenings that have taken place in one's life—particularly the earlier years of one's life. If one is not healed from a situation—emotionally, spiritually, and even mentally—before they are placed in key positions, then the choices made or influenced by them would have serious, negative repercussions.

A person who is involved in a relationship—a marriage or otherwise—who has been hurt through a divorce or breakup of some kind, or as a result of abuse or infidelity and has not been fully healed— will not truly accept or experience true love and all that it encompasses. It is highly likely that the next relationship will not last and even more likely that such a person will, in turn, hurt the one he/she is with— whether intentionally or unintentionally.

It is not difficult to discern that the atheists and those constantly attacking Christianity and its principles were hurt previously, and they were not healed; nor have they forgiven. So any decisions they make are influenced significantly by their experiences.

The crisis at this time globally, is that we have hurting people in key positions of influence and authority, making or influencing decisions that negatively affect a significant part of each nation.

A person who has been molested (male or female) in earlier years, for example, who may be placed in a position of authority such as law enforcement, lobby groups, or politics, and is not healed from that issue has the potential to do great damage to many!

Abortion

What would allow people to promote abortion? Abortion is what the Bible describes as Child Sacrifice. In fact, it is mentioned as one of the major reasons that the kingdom of Israel was destroyed by the Assyrians and the people exiled and enslaved. Abortion is the destruction of the helpless rather than their rescue. There is no difference among the cold-blooded murderer, the rapist, and the persons who push and support abortion (2 Kings 17:17–18).

When People Hurt

When people are not healed, their past influences their future, so they cannot move forward. Ultimately, in a sense, their future becomes their past! So growth is hindered from all angles.

A person in law enforcement, for example, may have experienced great injustices in his/her earlier years. It is quite possible that that person may have become a part of law enforcement to exact revenge on a particular person or a particular group of persons. It happens both locally and internationally.

With all the years of slavery and oppression of the black race, our black race needs to be healed! Look at Ferguson, Boston, Sanford, and even in Jamaica—people are hurt! Some don't have a father, and, oftentimes, many of them suffer great injustice. Based on the happenings, it seems that there are two different kinds of law meted out depending on who the perpetrators are—a law for the rich and another for the poor. Lotto scammers go to prison, and money launderers go free! This is the view of the people.

Most of our politicians today are hurting people who have not been healed—they have hurt/are now hurting other people. Many men who abuse women first saw it in their home or community, and any good teacher will tell you that they can look at a child and tell what is going on in their family. The sad thing is that, if God is the only One Whose Presence can bring total healing and He is being rejected by society in general, then we will inevitably see the increase of violence, stress, and hopelessness. Nothing can replace God and all that He does.

The Church is not exempt from this—any true Pastor will tell you as well: people who are hurt and refuse to forgive and be healed end up hurting themselves, their families, and the congregation and will be the first to run to the media to discredit or defame the Pastor and the Church.

There has to be healing for us to move forward as a people and a nation and experience the development, growth, and positive changes that come with that healing.

CHAPTER 30

WHY COMMIT SUICIDE?

The recent death of famous actor Robin Williams brings back into focus the levels of stress and depression that many go through, particularly (but not only) in the business profession, military, entertainment, and even pastoral/ministerial sectors; in other words, popular people on the front line!

The global economic system is now driving people into serious depression. Studies show that suicide rates are at extremely higher levels among males in comparison to the females.

Oftentimes, people equate a happy face with being OK and a sad or expressionless face with being down or depressed. It really takes discernment to recognize what is really happening in someone's life.

Most of the popular people often pretend that everything is OK, because they have to maintain a certain status or a certain persona in the presence of friends, colleagues, or those around them. Most often many readily receive from, but very few seek to give to them—the genuine care and even encouragement and true support they may need. Even fewer take the time to make that effort.

When persons fall on hard times, the very thought of being broke again, the fear of losing job, money, or assets, the loss of real estate, the fear of failure, and the loss of friends are almost devastating and extremely discouraging. All these can drive a person into depression and suicidal thoughts. Many will start to take drugs and/or alcohol to escape the realities they face. However, that is no real solution because it does more harm than good in every way!

Counseling Perspective

I have counseled many over the years—those who struggled with depression and suicide, as well as those who had fallen on hard times, and they often expressed that they felt like they no longer belonged to society. Others said they felt like a burden to their family, friends, and society. There were others that said that because they are no longer in the "limelight," their "friends" don't come around—this was especially so among those who were in high-ranking positions and were then separated (let go) from the organization. Those they once worked with passed them on the street as if they didn't know them! These are some of the things that drove them to the brink. They went through serious rejection.

On the flip side, there were those who, on their way up, pushed aside or "stepped on" some people, and when faced with the adversity, the guilt, embarrassment, and rejection overwhelmed them.

I always encourage people to keep simple friends—those who are willing to stand with you in good and bad. Those are true friends!

People will come around you when you are climbing and walk away if you fall, and when hard times come, people will see you as a burden, not as a blessing! Then you become the topic of their conversations! It is critical to have a positive spiritual foundation.

Do Not Commit Suicide!

Everything in life has its ups and downs. No season remains the same. Every situation has an expiration date! Always remember Job! He lost all, but he recovered twice the loss! Whatever you have lost, there is always the potential for you to recover far more. Your latter days have the potential to be greater than the former (Job 42:12).

Whatever doors close, remember that greater doors can open. Remember your life values far more than anything!

Committing suicide will not solve your problems! It will be the beginning of problems! There is nothing called *rest in peace* (RIP) when one commits suicide! Think about your loved ones! During your time of depression, don't focus on yourself; focus on helping other people. It was when Job prayed for his friends that his breakthrough and relief took place. Suicide is an act of murder! (Hebrews 10:26; Exodus 20:13; 1 Corinthians 3:16–17; 1 Corinthians 6:19–20; Hebrews 13:5–6). Committing suicide means you have rejected God's love and God's salvation.

Always remember that your struggle is a result of your purpose. Pray! Seek someone you confide in to speak with. Depression is a spirit (Isaiah 61:1–3). A simple thing such as praising or playing music that glorifies God can bring even immediate and positive change upon you.

You are a winner! You are not a loser! When problems come, all it is doing is revealing your capacity and potential and allowing you to see what is within you to come out! It is also revealing those who are true and genuine around you!

There are many who have lost everything, and they have come back greater, such as Colonel Sanders (KFC founder); R. H. Macy had several failed businesses before the mega chain Macy's became successful! Soichiro Honda was turned down by Toyota Motor Corporation for a job when he was interviewed to be an engineer. He was jobless for a long while, but then he started making scooters of his own at his home; and with the encouragement of his neighbors, he started his own business— thus Honda today!

Don't be afraid to start over!

Urgent Help Needed for Police and Soldiers

Every problem has an expiration date, and in life, one should never make a permanent decision based on a temporary situation. It is most distressing and even embarrassing each time there is a news break that a member of the security force has shot and killed their spouse and then turned the gun on himself. In addition to that, such action will cause many parents to discourage their daughters from connecting in any way with those in the armed/security forces!

Relationship issues are no respecter of persons, especially as it affects those in highly stressful work environments. While soldiers are trained to function under pressure and are taught to be emotionally hard, when temptation and disagreements come, they should realize that their families are not the true enemies and should seek immediate help! They should never allow their pride to destroy their lives and the lives of others.

There are many avenues available to get help:

- civilian Pastors
- force or military chaplains
- commissioned and non-commissioned officers
- family members
- respected individuals in the community

Those close to our armed services/police force members—both at work and at home—must quickly discern when there are issues and report it to the authorities at their place of work, and those in authority should not be quick to discharge them or allow them to have a loss of pay. Oftentimes, it is in fact financial issues that are at the root of their problems. In other cases, it could be insecurity. Most, because of the long hours away from their families, dread the very thought of infidelity taking place with their spouse, and their colleagues would merciless taunt them if that should happen. Others are fearful of not sexually satisfying their spouse as a result of the stressful situations within which they work. Most times their spouses are unable to deal with their transition from civilian to military/force lifestyle and often feel trapped and in bondage, particularly since those in the military/force have been trained in intelligence gathering. So, oftentimes, the spouse would confide in someone whom they don't realize has the wrong motive, and that ultimately leads to infidelity, which in many cases can lead to fatalities.

I have always said—and this is only my personal view—there is no way military personnel should be on the streets for long periods, carrying out police work! Soldiers are trained to kill, and to have soldiers for a long period carrying out patrol duties can lead to more stress and frustration. Many of them don't have the patience to handle civil matters on that scale, because that was not their training.

Solutions

- There is a global neglect of security personnel. Most, after they serve, are put out on the street; some fall on hard times, are in need, and are without medical attention. Others find it hard to transition back to civilian life.
- There are many things that can be done to help our military and police personnel to reduce fatalities—whether they are currently serving.
- Have more spiritual support—having devotions on base for soldiers and police personnel.
- Have more rest, recreation, and relaxation for members and their families together.
- Have duty-free opportunities for members bringing in their barrels, etc., at the airports.
- Offer work experience in the public or private sector for those who are close to retirement. This will help them to transition.
- Have free education at all levels for the children of our soldiers and police personnel.
- Utilize the Reserves to carry out all duties the regular forces would carry out on the weekends to allow the regular soldiers to rest.
- Have better scheduling of police personnel and implement/increase volunteer policing or home guards utilizing ex-members and business professionals to reduce the work pressure on police personnel.
- Companies should reach out by assisting security personnel with spa treatments (for relaxation), groceries, or time at our beautiful

resorts for themselves and their families, and set up more exchange programs with our international allies and partners to train overseas. There can be two-week training sessions to gain working knowledge and learn about different cultures.

- Increase housing loans for members to acquire homes and allow them easier access for that. The living standards for those who have chosen to risk life and limb in these professions are below what we would willingly accept!

There are many who would quickly criticize the security forces of the nation as corrupt. Do they know what they have to undergo, especially in a failed society? Do they know what they have to work with, the lack of resources all-round, and the treatment they undergo?

Muster! Called to Warfare!

As soldiers, in the same way that we are trained to fight naturally, there is a spiritual battle that we must also fight. "The weapons of our warfare are not carnal, but mighty through God to the pulling down of strongholds" (2 Corinthians 10:4). Strongholds in this context refer to anything opposing God's will for your life and family. Ephesians 6:12 reminds us that "we wrestle not against flesh and blood . . ." Hence, carnal wars and worldly weapons will not do! We need weapons empowered by God to give us victory as soldiers. Remember, once you are trained as a soldier in the natural, there is no retirement; you are always a soldier! We must always be ready and always be second to none!

In the same way that you would dress in full battle order while on patrol or in war, the Lord wants us to dress in full armor spiritually. There is no leave or retirement for us! The enemy still wants to ambush us and our family members and loved ones.

God has been speaking to many past and present military personnel in dreams/visions. Sometimes He will show you visions with you mustering, and sometimes He will show you yourself mustering in fatigue/camouflage.

When He shows that to you, then you must be on the alert. Pray for your family and yourself, and if you are an officer, pray for the men under your command! The Holy Spirit always communicates with military people in military ways. For example, if He shows you yourself in ceremonial dress, it means something official or business. Also, when He shows you a pistol, it means close combat fighting and that it is a close enemy. Rifles indicate that the battle is from afar. If He shows you a military vehicle, it means the nation or your work environment. When He shows you your personal vehicle, it speaks of you and your family. When He shows you your past house, past vehicle, past school, then it indicates that some past enemies are in action and in sniper mode.

Further to that, never take the following symbols lightly:

- broken teeth
- raven
- bullets/ammunition
- alligators
- snakes
- someone kissing you

Watch your twelve o'clock and your six o'clock!

Signs and symbols are very important, and it is equally important for us to take note or heed. They can save your life, the life of your comrade in arms, as well as the lives of your family and children.

While I prayed, the Lord revealed that many soldiers—past and present—are coming up against battles because of past choices. Some are against our own comrades, neighbors, or past relationships that went sour. It could be that someone is angry with you and set a trap for your demise. Many times it is a matter of soldiers who got involved in witchcraft, or others employed the use of "guards" to protect them and it backfired. Hence, we are called to fight in the spiritual and natural daily. Fighting in the spiritual realm can avert tragedy for you and your family.

There are many things you can do to stop the manifestation of what is revealed to you that would work adversely against you and your family. You can go on a three-day fast or a ten-day fast—vegetables and water only—and ask God to avert it and bind it. Ensure you pray for your children daily—regardless of their age. Something happens when men pray! We have greater authority, and as fathers, we have the authority to bless and to curse! When the enemy cannot get you, they will go after your children. Ask the Lord to put a hedge of protection around you and your family daily.

Remember, you must war spiritually for your faith, family, finance, community, and nation! We will never outgrow warfare; we must learn to adapt.

As you arise each day, pray this prayer according to Exodus 33:14, Psalm 91, and Psalm 103:21:

> Father, in the name of Jesus, we come to You right now.
> According to Psalm 91, cover me, my family, and my household each
>   day
> From gunmen, knifemen, terrorists, snipers, ambush, or friendly fire
> As well as past and present enemies.
> Give me discernment and keep me in a state of readiness
> To maneuver and to be ready when the enemy comes.
> Keep my weapons in a state of readiness—they will not malfunction.
> Help me always to remember my marksmanship principle.
> Release Your Divine angels to assist me, Jehovah Tsebaoth.
> Jehovah Shammah, let Your Presence cover me always and expose
>   any spies.
> Cover me with Your blood and release all Your ministering angels.
> Be with me always to instill tactics and strategies.
> In Jesus' name—Victory! Amen.

ENCOURAGEMENT
FOR THE FAMILY

CHAPTER 31

BACK TO CORE VALUES

When money, fame, and power take precedence over core values and morals among the people of a nation, the nation is on its way to becoming degenerate and corrupt.

Over the past fifty years, we have been subjected to various forms of indiscipline at all levels; many have been sucking the nation dry of its resources and beauty. It is time for things to change. But the change can't come until there is a return to core values!

Respect and honor must be shown, first, to God, and then to our leaders and to each other.

The treatment of leaders during the various inquiries and the past elections has brought a curse on the nation.

Public apologies and healing must take place within the nation. Regardless of the number of financial strategies put in place, political instability and erosion of the nation's foundation will continue!

Simple Principles

So we need to get back to basics. Simple things such as saying "Good morning" or "Good afternoon" to those we pass should begin again. Furthermore,

- Always address people by their titles: Mr., Mrs., Your Honor, Sergeant, Colonel, President, Prime Minister, Rev., and so on. Never use the term "you guys" when addressing your leaders/ those above you in a conversation with them.
- Always have respect for a person's office (position). You may think they are unworthy of the position, but they are in positions of authority, and should you one day be in a position of authority, the treatment you issue will be the same treatment that meets you!
- Regardless of the relationship (or lack of one), address your mother and father with respect when speaking to them— especially if you desire to have long life!
- Say "please," "excuse me," and "thank you."
- Don't enter a person's office, home, or room without being invited to do so.
- Don't take a seat unless invited to do so.
- (Men) Don't pray or eat with your head covered; once you enter a building, remove your hat (or headgear) as a sign of reverence/ respect.
- (Women) When you are in an interview, dress appropriately (nothing too tight, too short, or too long). Sit with your legs together.
- (Men) Unless otherwise instructed, dress professionally for interviews. Do not wear your pants with your underpants exposed or with the waist of your pants below your buttocks. That style is prison wear.
- Stop using the phones during church services and any other formal functions and gatherings; it shows a lack of respect for God and for those around you.

- Get back to the dining table! There are many of our young people who do not know basic table manners. Some don't know how to use a knife and fork, how to sit at the table, or that they shouldn't eat and talk at the same time!
- Stop chewing gum while talking; it is poor manners.
- (Young people) When in public (transportation or buildings), always offer a seat to elders, pregnant women, and those with disabilities.
- Always speak to law enforcement personnel with respect (whether they do the same to you). It works in your favor at all times!
- Never be disrespectful to officials or ex-officials. You never know what tomorrow may bring.
- Bring order back and form a line when you are in groups waiting. Some people refuse to do it locally, but if it is required overseas, they eagerly do so.

Flag Protocol

The flag represents a living country and is itself considered a living thing.

- It must be displayed in a manner where all parts/colors symbolic can be seen.
- It must not touch the ground or floor.
- It should not be draped over vehicles; only by military personnel, police, or state officials.
- It must not be flown during rain and must not be folded when wet.
- A salute should be given when the flag is raised or lowered. Furthermore, when the anthem is played and the flag is displayed, all will stand at attention.
- The flag must always be used in a dignified manner.

If we—whether public official, the media, or John Q. Public—refuse to respect ourselves, each other, and our nation, no one else will. Other nations will disrespect us and ignore our sovereignty.

We must get back to basics.

Use the Bible for Values and Attitudes

Why are we alarmed at the breaking down of values and attitudes within the society, when the Book of codes, ethics, morals, and values has been disregarded and rejected? Why waste more money on research to find out why our children behave the way they do? We have replaced the Bible with *Harry Potter*, X-rated cartoons, and other forms of media that teach our children how to perform magic, engage in violence, and tolerate un-Godly behavior. Media and marketing companies engage in borderline pornography just to advertise hair oil, food, and drink!

The family, which is the first line of government, must get back in position and begin to train the children. There are codes of ethics and moral standards in the Bible for both Christians and non-Christians.

With the fight to remove the Bible from our society, what do we replace it with? Will it be the Quran, New Age doctrines, the principles of Kabballah or Kundalini—what will it be?

Surprisingly, even media houses are afraid to quote scriptures. They prefer to quote from philosophers of all kinds and doctrines of all kinds—Monotheism, Pantheism, Astrology, Gnosticism, Universalism and Spiritualism. All of these "isms" may lead to Communism!

It is interesting and somewhat hypocritical that when officials are being sworn in or when we are taking oaths in a court of law, the Bible is the book on which the hands are placed to make the vow that they are to honor. Do they realize that the oath made with the hand on the Bible means that it is a vow to uphold, not just the constitution but also everything contained in the Bible? When people are afraid to uphold what is within the Book, it is the equivalent to perjury and treason—especially when they vow to "tell the truth, the whole truth, and nothing but the truth, so help me God."

Code of Ethics

There are scriptures that speak about the labor laws, severance pay, firing employees, rotation of workers, particularly through Deuteronomy 15:13–14, Deuteronomy 23:25–26, Deuteronomy 24:14–15, Leviticus

19:13, Leviticus 25:43, and 1 Kings 4:27. The scriptures also teach us not to oppress employees and not to rob them in their salaries/pay (James 5).

The scriptures also tell us that foreigners are to be given labor jobs and the citizens are to be given the management of the labor force. The Bible is also clear on gender issues and human rights.

The scriptures speak to us on environmental issues, warning us not to cut down fruit trees, what to do with bodily waste, resting the land, dealing with toxic waste, and having open spaces for beautification of the town. It also lays down the principles of the 3 Rs—recycle, reuse, and reduce (Numbers 35:1–6; Deuteronomy 20:19; Deuteronomy 23:13–15; Leviticus 25:1–7; Psalm 104:10–14).

The scriptures teach us about the Law of Gleaning—a mandate given by God for every businessperson and every farmer to set aside a part of their budget to help the poor (Leviticus 19:9–10). Both rich and poor need each other! There are certain blessings the rich cannot receive until they help the poor, especially healing, Divine revelations, and new ideas!

Leviticus 19:32 speaks to us about how we must treat an elder— it is shameful and disrespectful to call them dinosaurs, ignoring their deathbed pleas for assistance, robbing them of their pensions, or holding on to their pensions so that they can't even purchase food and medication after they have labored within and for their nation!

Leviticus 19:15 speaks to us about the fact that we are not to honor the mighty while we bring injustice to the poor!

Leviticus 19:29 says, "Do not prostitute your daughter, to cause her to be a harlot, lest the land fall into harlotry, and the land become full of wickedness."

Leviticus 19:35–36, Exodus 23:7, Proverbs 11:1, and Zechariah 8:16–17 speak of integrity in business. There should be no selling of old stock for new stock prices; selling inferior products; "marrying" items, false advertising, and deceptive marketing strategies; lying press releases; and falsifying financial statements.

Leviticus 20:2 clearly tells us how *not* to treat our children.

The Bible clearly tells us that when morality breaks down within a nation, crime and violence, bad economy, poor values and attitudes, and low moral standards will result. Joel 1 and 2 tells us the causes and solutions concerning the issues of the nation. The Bible even tells us about animal rights.

Application of the Biblical principles can save us a great deal of the struggles we now endure.

CHAPTER 32

CHOICES DETERMINE SUCCESS

We are in an era where the choices we make are critical to our success in accomplishing our goals and objects—individually and nationally. The survival of businesses and nations are directly connected to the choices made by all involved.

The word *choice* simply means "the opportunity, ability, or power to choose between different things." Choices do not affect only one person; it can affect an entire generation.

Everyone is given the freewill to make choices. There is no such thing as "no other choice," because as long as there is God, there is always a way. Choices must be based therefore on God's Word, His instructions, and truth!

Choices can make or break you. There are many who made choices in their youth but now regret making those choices and have to live with the consequences of their actions. Some persons chose the wrong spouse or business partner; others embarked on the wrong career path and made bad investments. Further to that, some followed the wrong leader or chose the wrong group to call friends and are living with the consequences.

Remember this: choices should never be made in haste. They must be made in prayer and fasting. Whatever choices we make in any area have consequences—both negative and positive. Most people don't like to wait or be patient, but waiting reveals the hearts, strengthens and matures you, and increases your knowledge. Most importantly, it removes any potential danger. Most people want to be successful so quickly that they make choices that bring failure and pain. True success comes through hardship, suffering, and patience.

Right and Wrong Choices

We must be careful making choices through peer pressure. Choices must be made based on facts and faith! Right choices will separate you from wrong friends and associates! People make wrong choices because of fame and popularity, because they are making them by sight! Oftentimes when persons are given the option of more than one job opportunity, they choose the job that offers a higher salary, only to find stress and failure along the way. The refuse the job that has a lower salary but better long-term benefits and, as a result, miss a greater opportunity for upward mobility!

This tells us, therefore, that our choices should not be made by focusing solely on how lucrative it is—how much money can be had—but, instead, by looking also at the intangible benefits.

I have seen women pray to marry a rich man, and God sends a poor man whom He would ultimately make a millionaire, and they reject him because he turned up poor. They made the choice of rejecting that person because they looked at his present circumstances and did not see his potential for greatness. Choices should not be made based on present circumstances.

Desperation should not be the basis for your decision-making, because that can cost you dearly!

There is a great deal of suffering, wasting of precious resources, and general failure with regard to political choices made worldwide. Some made choices based on age, gender, skin color, and oratorical abilities—the eloquence of a speaker. This should not be the basis for choosing a national leader. Such choices should be made on the basis of truth, integrity, and willingness to be a servant-leader and obey the voice of God; someone who will champion the rights and needs of the poor. Family must be such a leader's number-one priority! Such a leader must be willing to embrace new ideas and new ways of thinking and also be willing and ready to unite the people across political lines.

Remember that the choices you make can put you either five years ahead or five years behind.

Ten Keys for Improving Your Quality of Life

1. Appreciate the gift of life that has been given to you! That you are alive is a miracle and a gift. Appreciate the love of God that sustains you and extends to you grace, mercy, and great favor. Don't forget to appreciate what others do for you—especially when it helps to alleviate even the smallest problem/issue you have been experiencing. In all these instances, remember to say "Thank you!" (Psalm 100:4; Romans 1:21; Colossians 3:15).

2. Respect yourself enough to represent Christ well through your attire, your attitude, and your actions! Like it or not, self-respect is mainly, if not only, evident through your external/outward expressions! Show respect to those set over you. How you address or deal with those set over you at work or in ministry is important, regardless of how they treat you! (Genesis 16:1–10; I Samuel 24:3–7; I Timothy 6: 1–2). The more you choose to address those set over you with respect, the greater your reward will be, because you would be following the principles of God, which He will ultimately honor, and you will also be setting good examples for the generation after you to follow.

3. Empathize with those around you, particularly in difficult situations and times (Romans 12:9–11). You may not know exactly what they may be feeling or going through, but extend a hand, spend some time, or give some words of encouragement and let them know that despite all, you feel their hurt/pain and that you feel for them. It is easy to avoid people going through painful situations—especially if they are surrounded by others

and especially when you really don't know what to say. But even saying "I don't know what to say to ease this pain, but I'm here for you" can go such a long way!

4. Care! Care genuinely about others. Don't be afraid to let someone know that you care—about their welfare, their situation, them, and the things that are significant to them! (Hebrews 13:1; 1 Corinthians 12:24–26). Furthermore, you must ensure that there are no ulterior motives attached to your care! A pure heart and mind are key to truly caring about someone. This compels us to always seek the Lord for a pure heart and for His love to dwell in us. If you truly care, you will not run when adversity hits them. If you truly care, you will not walk away when you are experiencing the blessings while they have not yet come into their season of blessings (Galatians 6:1–6).

5. Pursue God through Jesus Christ and the things of God, and you will never lose your way! God is Love, and He exudes and exemplifies holiness, peace, righteousness, faith, patience, and gentleness! Pursue these things and pursue the things that will edify another! (Romans 14:19; 1 Corinthians 14:1; 1 Thessalonians 5:15; 1 Timothy 6:11; 2 Timothy 2:22; Hebrews 12:14; 1 Peter 3:11). These all allow us to experience the goodness of God and the kind of joy that can only come from God by the power of His Holy Spirit!

6. Submit yourself to God, to the principles and instructions of God, and to God's Word! (James 4:7). As you do this, He will open to you ways of escape from trouble, solutions, and new ideas, and your faith and trust in Him will increase. As a result, you will learn to hear His voice and understand how He relates to you and how immensely He loves you! You will learn and understand what it means to truly love and also how to receive love!

7. Love the Lord God with your whole being and strength—with everything within you! (Deuteronomy 6:5). Don't be afraid to express your love to Him—through your obedience to His Word and His instructions, through your worship of Him without inhibitions, through praise without hesitation, and through the frequency and level of intensity of your communication with Him!

Never be afraid to express love to God your Creator and Father. Remember also to love your neighbor as you do yourself and owe no man anything but love! (Matthew 19:19; Romans 13:8). Remember to love yourself because you are made perfectly and with great respect (Psalm 139).

8. Meditate on the Lord and Word of God daily! Don't try to "clear your mind" and that sort of nonsense—that is not what the Lord tells us to do (Joshua 1:8; Psalm 1:2; Psalm 63:6; Psalm 77:12; Psalm 119; Psalm 143:5). Recognize that you can never truly "clear" your mind—that is a deception! The Lord instructs us to meditate on His Word—think about His Word and "digest" them with our minds! Keep them at the forefront of your thoughts so that we can execute them daily. Meditate on God's Word because they are life to our spirit!

9. Communicate! Take the time to communicate with God in prayer (Matthew 21:22). Spend time with God, not only to tell Him all about your troubles but also to spend time to listen to Him, because He will speak to your spirit and refresh and strengthen you! Your relationship with Him will strengthen as your communication with Him increases! Furthermore, communicate with those you love! Don't assume they know should know or should understand you! Talk to each other and make every effort to facilitate two-way exchanges and dialogues.

10. Give! Always remember that your giving is the opportunity God gives you to receive the very blessings or solutions for which you have asked Him. God operates according to His own principles of sowing and reaping! He also honors His Word! (Genesis 8:22; Psalm 107:37). As you sow/give into His work, He will cause you to receive even greater than you expect. But recognize that this principle is not a lottery game. Don't give today and expect a windfall tomorrow! While He is more than capable of doing so, He gives you a harvest in the time of your greatest need! When you give to the work of the Lord, it's one of the best investments you could ever make! You are helping to alleviate the needs of others while obeying God's word and instructions, and, as a result, a double blessing awaits you in your time of greatest need.

Value Your Life and Fulfill Your Purpose

Let us all give thanks for the most important thing—life! Let us also give thanks to the One Who gives us life—Jesus Christ!

Typically at the end of a calendar year, there are many mixed emotions. Some have financial woes, others have lost loved ones throughout the year, yet others are uncertain of what the future holds. Many are unable to physically be with family members because of circumstances beyond their control. Some may be in the hospital or on the street at this time. Some may have money, but they are lonely. However, regardless of the circumstances that exist, we must remember to do two of the most important things we can do in this life: 1) value your life and (2) fulfill your purpose.

Many want to give up hope now, and, to many, it seems as if darkness is overcoming light, and hopelessness and joblessness are taking the lead. But one of the reasons that this is happening is that people are not fulfilling their purpose.

We are all unique and were created to solve problems. When we refuse to walk in our purpose, then we lose, and we are denying the world of the solutions that we were created to solve.

Have you ever asked yourself the question, "Am I in the wrong field/career?" Have you ever asked the question, "What is my purpose in life?"

What are the things that make you happy? What makes you sad? Why am I going through the things I go through in life? All of these are clues to your purpose! Why do you seem to hate injustice more passionately than the other person? Maybe your calling is law! Why does it hurt you more deeply than the next person when someone you don't even know has been badly hurt, abused, or killed? It could be that your calling is an advocate or a health professional! Do you have a vehement passion for the corruption you see or for the economic problems you see happening, and others around you think you are going overboard with you passionate discussions? It could be that your calling is in the political arena or in economic policy making!

Step over the Hindrances

One of the greatest obstacles and hindrances in our lives is often ourselves! Faith without works is dead! Don't just criticize and talk for the sake of talking. Do something constructive and make this world a better place. Utilize the gifts that God has given you, as well as the resources, and touch someone's life. You can be a mentor to someone. Help an abandoned child! Show love to someone's child! The cemetery is filled with unfulfilled purposes and unexpressed ideas.

Begin to cut down on waste—and start with your household first! Cut down on entertainment, the use of electricity, wasting food, gambling, the use of alcohol, and even the use of A/C in the car. Use some the savings to help the less fortunate. We must lead by example. By doing this, we are demonstrating the love of God! The Word of God says that when we give to the poor, we lend to the Lord, and the Lord is looking for lenders!

Goals and Objectives for You

Every decision we make must be tied to the value of life! So let your goals and objectives include some of the following:

- Edify someone each day.
- Take the time to be in the Presence of God each day. He needs relationships, not one-night stands. This is where you will find/ receive the solutions, healing, and how to make better choices.
- Evaluate your stewardship and see where the pitfalls are so that you can be a better person/leader.
- Sow good seed on a daily basis—quality time, talents, and so on, knowing that you reap the harvest of whatever seed you sow.
- Maintain a forgiving heart—let no bitterness dwell in you.
- Ensure that whatever plans you have, God is a part of those plans.
- Be thankful and appreciate those around you.

CHAPTER 33

CHRISTIANS, WALK IN
YOUR AUTHORITY

As the world continues to plunge into darkness—sexual immorality, lawlessness, crime, violence, corruption, hatred, racism, and all kinds of debauchery—the secular religion has been coming to the forefront to encourage Christians to conform to that way of life. Thus, the goal is that Christians must be tolerant of the immoral activities and lifestyles, but those who engage in such activities and lifestyle will remain intolerant of Christians and the message and name of Jesus Christ!

Every Christian is given the authority by God to make a change within their environment. Christianity is the only faith to which God has given authority to dominate in the earth. Luke 10:19 says, "Behold, I give you the authority to trample on serpents and scorpions, and over all the power of the enemy, and nothing shall by any means hurt you."

God has given Christians authority—why is this authority not being utilized?

We as Christians have the authority to decree and declare, to bind and to loose, and even to overturn un-Godly decrees! Every believer has the right to sit as a shareholder on the heavenly council as an intercessor. We are judge, jury, and sheriffs within the earth on spiritual matters. We have the authority to decide with our prayer, fasting, votes, money, and sphere of influence that rule over us. Believers must stop allowing the secular leaders to bring heresy to them concerning the separation of Church and state.

Some of the chaos taking place globally is the result of the complacency and passivity of believers. The Enemy knows the Word more than many believers do. Those who are prophets of God have the authority and the power of words within their mouths (Jeremiah 1:9–10).

God has given Christians authority over nations and kingdoms to subdue every aggressive satanic force.

The Reflection in the Earth

The happenings we are seeing within the earth are a reflection of the Church. Many Christians are now giving excuses or trying to be "politically correct." Many say that we should just let things roll as they are because God will soon come, or God is in control, or the Bible must be fulfilled. But the Bible specifically tells Christians to occupy and do business until His return. He commanded Christians to make disciples of the nations. Nowhere in the Bible did the Lord tell Christians to stop doing what He commanded us to do when these things happen. Neither did He tell Christians to turn a blind eye.

If Christians don't exercise their God-given authority, then soon they will wake up to full enslavement by the enemy! The scripture 2 Corinthians 6 tells us that Christians have the authority to judge the world, judge angels, and that is why we must support each other, not to take each other to court. If every Christian would fast at least one time per week for positive global change and for God's glory to manifest in every institution, and for God to raise up righteous leaders and lawmakers, and to ask God for souls to be saved; give up one meal and give it to the homeless/poor; cut down their time on social media and remain loyal to God more than they are to their denomination; then we would already have the revival the earth needs and is seeking.

Battles Christians Fight Daily

It is not easy to be a Christian. Every Christian must know that our fight is not against each other physically but is a spiritual fight! Christians should not be paranoid or ignorant of spiritual warfare. Wherever you work, live, or socialize, there is always a constant battle to get you out! So we have to fight to stay in love with God and maintain our salvation—to maintain our purity, to maintain your faith and belief, to maintain your marriage and family, and to maintain your integrity and your finances and your very focus!

We are spiritual beings in flesh. We come against strongholds on a daily basis. That is why, as believers, we cannot hold on to humanistic or philosophical views. Everything that happens in the physical is a result of spiritual happenings. The enemy does not want the Christian to know the truth or have any form of depth in God. He wants us to be at a place where every wind of doctrine blows us away. Christians need to walk in their God-given authority.

Keys on How to Receive Your Miracle

1) Obey the voice of God (Deuteronomy 28).
2) Follow the instruction of the Lord (1 Samuel 15:22).
3) Obey His prophets and prosper (2 Chronicles 20:20).
4) Fast—various fasts: Daniel, Esther (Isaiah 58; Esther 3–4).
5) Pray always (1 Thessalonians 5:17).
6) Worship the Lord (2 Chronicles. 20:21–22).
7) Sow seed to deal with different issues (Genesis 8:22).
8) Be full of *faith*, not fear (Hebrews 11).
9) In addition to faith, put works in place (James 2).
10) Believe God's instructions without doubt! (2 Kings 6:24–33; 2 Kings 7:1–2; 2 Kings 5:9–14 [through the prophets]).
11) Know that the anointing in the hand of the man of God will bring deliverance and miracles when he places his hand on something (2 Kings 13:14–16).

12) Recognize that obedience to the instructions of a prophet of God does mighty things in the spiritual and also that for deliverance from your enemies to come, you must be persistent! (2 Kings 13:18).

13) Holiness! Repent at all times! (Psalm 51).

Twelve Commandments for Your Breakthrough!

1) *Trust* God always (Proverbs 3:5; Psalm 37:3).
2) Always have *faith* in God! (Hebrews 11; Luke 17:6).
3) Always *sow* a seed! (Genesis 8:22; Genesis 26).
4) Trust God's *timing*! (Ecclesiastes 3).
5) *Seek* God continuously! (Matthew 6:33).
6) *Believe* in the vision God has given you (Habakkuk 2).
7) *Remember*, God gives you power to get wealth, not man! (Deuteronomy 8:18).
8) *Call* upon Him! (Jeremiah 33:3).
9) *Repent* daily! (Psalm 51).
10) *Confess* the Word! (Psalm 1; Psalm 23; Joshua 1:8; Psalm 103)
11) Speak to your mountains! (Mark 11:12–24)
12) Continue to *encourage* someone during your testing! (Galatians 6:2)

Miracles Are in Your Mouth! Speak!

Not everyone is a prophet. However, everyone has the ability to prophesy or speak words that would bring change!

If God created the universe by speaking words and we are made in His image, then we, too, have the capacity to speak our very future into being! Every word we speak, good or bad, will bring forth a harvest. We must decide what harvest we want.

First, God wants us to begin speaking positive words to cancel all the negative words we have spoken about ourselves or that others have spoken about us (Proverbs 16:23–24).

Confessing positive words brings healing and peace, creates light and life, and builds our self-esteem. It brings hope and creates a new path for us. It brings victory!

Proverbs 18:21 lets us know that a person's life largely reflects the fruit of his/her tongue. To speak life is to speak God's perspective on any issue of life. To declare anything negative is declaring death and reinjects the past into your current situation.

We will be held accountable for every idle word we speak on a daily basis. The negative words we speak will determine whether we are righteous or we are condemned.

Many times we see people suffering, and it is the result of what they speak about themselves (Matthew 12:36–37).

The tongue causes defilement and brings strife, war, sickness, and curses. The Word of God even tells us that we can tame animals, but the tongue is more difficult to tame and releases poison. Many die, never recovering from this poison.

A negative or untamed tongue is controlled by a python spirit. Many churches, families, and organizations break up because of the tongue. God wants us to use our tongues to create miracles and to change our environment as well as to bless our children! In the same way that fear is a spirit, faith is a spirit!

When the spies gave a negative report, based on the giants they saw in the Land of Promise, it nearly destroyed the entire camp. Your negative words can become the trap that destroys you. Jesus shows us that there is power in our tongue. He showed this to us in Mark 11, when He spoke to the fig tree to dry up from the root and it did!

There are many things and cycles against which we need to speak! There are curses that need to dry up from the root, and we have the capacity to make it happen. There are contrary winds and storms that tend to come against us but which we can speak against to stop them from coming in our direction. Within your mouth, you have the power to remove any obstacle coming against you (Zechariah 4:6–7). We are children of grace, and we have the authority within our mouths to remove or speak against any opposition.

God wants us to find a scripture of promise and begin to declare it daily! (Hebrews 11:3; Genesis 1).

Joel 3:10 reminds us that the weak should say they are strong, and if words create the environment, we can create a Godly environment for us and our families.

Declare these words today!

I am blessed!
I am walking in favor!
I am walking in power!
I am walking in victory!
I am approved and access is granted!
I am brilliant!
I will make it!
I am a champion!
I am beloved!
I am beautiful/handsome!
I am motivated!
I am strong!
I am forgiven!
I am rich!
I am a billionaire!
I am prosperous!
I am able!

Understanding Dreams and Visions

Many people are getting dreams and visions today, but they don't understand them. Signs and symbols are critical to our knowing what God is saying in these last days. God is speaking to us clearly of things to come for both leaders and individuals.

Hearing God's voice is a benefit that we are all able to receive; even those who are not believers in God. He speaks to us on a daily basis about changing our lives and accepting His Son, Jesus Christ (John 3:16; Acts 2:17–18; Revelation 3:20).

God speaks to us in dreams and visions, the written Word, through prophetic utterances, circumstances, and the suffering we go through. He can even use movies and His servants.

God *does not* speak to us through mediums or psychics; neither does God charge a fee for a service. People can bless the ministry but not to pay for a word. The Holy Spirit is not for sale! Neither must His Spiritual gifts be prostituted.

Keys to Hearing God's Voice

- Meet with the Lord regularly.
- Keep a journal of the things the Lord says to you, and wait for it to come to pass.
- Listen for the Word of the Lord and what He will say to you.
- Look for Him to speak to you in dreams and visions.

Understanding Symbols

God speaks to us through symbols. To better understand symbols when He speaks to us, we must first consult the Word of God to interpret the symbols. Both symbols and colors carry a message. For example, in the books of Genesis and Daniel, symbols and colors are critical. They were pertinent for the kings' dreams to be interpreted (Daniel 2, Genesis 40–41, Psalm 78:2).

Dreams and visions must be taken very seriously. Don't let anyone try to convince you that it is not important. If clearly understood, it can bring great blessing; if ignored, it can bring great disaster (Judges 7:10–15; Job 33:14–15; Genesis 39:21).

Here are some of the symbols and colors that show up frequently in dreams and visions: scales, schools, corn, a kiss, snakes, swords, flood, dogs, rainbow, school bus, alligator/crocodile, doves, dragons, cars, airplane, and fruits.

CHAPTER 34

YOUR PAST DOES NOT DETERMINE YOUR FUTURE

The world's ways are designed to judge a person and determine his/her future by looking at his/her past. This is particularly clear in the business sector and the credit system. Furthermore, this is also found to be true about the media. Additionally, those running for political office are often at the mercy of the media, who never fail to "dig up dirt" on those running for office to keep those matters at the forefront of the public eye and use it against them. The question here then is, what does one's past have to do with one's future? Everybody has a past, but a past does not determine one's future. Neither does one's past determine one's present. When a person wants to use your past to make certain decisions about your future, then he/she is automatically "playing God."

Regardless of the following choices a person may have made in the past, for example, it does not determine his/her future:

- prostitution
- promiscuity (multiple sex partners)
- drug/alcohol addiction

- homosexuality/lesbianism
- theft
- bad credit
- bankruptcy
- prison sentence

The moment that person repents, then they are forgiven—God remembers it no more (1 John 1:9).

If God's system was anything like the world system, then no one would be alive today. Interestingly, if the pasts of the individuals and groups attempting to condemn others using their past should come to light, many would be surprised and, I dare say, shocked!

Never let your past become your future. God is the only One Who controls your future. There is no vehicle that can drive in both reverse and forward!

Many times in a relationship, one party will ask the other to come clean before marriage takes place (and sometimes after). When one comes clean, the other tends not to forgive or they will use it to manipulate or curse the other person, and this leads to a breakdown in relationship. What if God should deal with us that way? If we don't pass our past, then we have no future (Isaiah 43:18–19).

God is always doing a new thing—new mercies each day, new grace, new supply, and new opportunities.

Sadly, our politicians and many church leaders keep bringing up the past. Many continually compare our current leaders to past leaders despite the fact that circumstances, situations, and eras have changed. There is a reason for an Old Testament and a New Testament. The Old dealt with the Law; the New deals with Grace and the future! Some are stuck in the Law—so much so that they have no room for grace! The 1950s, '60s, and '70s will not return!

The Purpose of the Past

Our past is not to be a weapon against us! The past must be used as a teacher of wisdom and a giver of experience. Focus more on the new things God is doing with your life. If you focus more on the past, you will not discern the new things. One who focuses on the past

- cannot walk by faith;
- will not forgive and remains embittered and hurt;
- walks with baggage, which hinders them walking into their future; or
- blinds you from embracing true friends and genuine love.

Our young people are seriously struggling because no future is being built for them. The time is being wasted on living in and from the past and fixing the present!

When you have been hurt and have not let go of that hurt, then when Mr./Ms. Right comes, you will reject him/her.

When you have been hurt in the church, then when a true shepherd comes, you will reject him/her.

Embrace the Future!

- Find scriptures in the Bible that speak about the future and confess them daily.
- Write down all your dreams and visions, goals and objectives, and wait for the manifestation.
- Never allow fear or failure to discourage you from walking into the future.
- Spiritual advancement requires faith! Unbelief will never see beyond the difficulties.
- Unbelief sees giants, mountains, and the past. Faith sees the future!
- Faith sees the greatness of God to accomplish the future in our lives! So it is time to confront the giants and obstacles that keep you in the dark and in the past!
- Your future is great! Don't allow any negative person, group, or circumstance to discourage you concerning your future!

God always uses your obstacles to promote you!

The Danger of Looking Back

Isaiah 43:18–19 says, "Do not remember the former things, nor consider the things of old. Behold, I will do a new thing, now it shall spring forth; shall you not know it? I will even make a road in the wilderness and rivers in the desert."

One cannot move ahead while looking back. No vehicle can go backward and forward at the same time. The Bible outlines that losers and failure are those who look back and dwell in the past, and when we dwell in the past, fear, bitterness, and unforgiveness persist! We must only use our past as a tool for learning and gaining wisdom. When we make mistakes, we are not to dwell on it and beat up on ourselves. Once we have truly repented, He never uses our past actions to judge us. Only evil people, the media, and politicians tend to use people's past to judge them. Our past does not determine our future; therefore, it should not be used to hold you at ransom!

There are many times persons see themselves in dreams/visions reversing a vehicle or looking in their rearview mirror. That is a signal that God is trying to tell us that we are looking back in the past. When a person continually looks back to the past, he/she is poised to backslide and as such is making the past his/her future! The failure of the Israelites was their continual looking back to and yearning for the things from which God had already delivered them.

Looking back to the past keeps you from focusing on the positive and from the blessings ahead where the prosperity and even greater things await! Even nations are unable to move forward because they keep looking back. The past must only be used for the sake of history and archiving.

Focus Ahead

Philippians 3:13–15 encourages us to forget those things that are behind and reach forward to those things that are ahead! What is ahead is *always* greater than what is behind.

The goal that is set for us, the prize, promotion, blessings, and benefits, are always ahead! Every mature person must renew his/her mind and press forward toward the goals and objectives set or us. Reach forward! The image is that of a runner on a course straining every muscle as he runs toward the goal—his hands stretched out to grasp the baton. Just think of someone running a 4 X 100 meter relay—USA vs. Jamaica. The runner cannot run forward while looking behind. He/She can't think about how badly he/she did yesterday or the medal he/she lost yesterday. A true champion has to get up and press ahead toward the mark. A boxer wouldn't stay down on the canvas; he/she has to get up and press forward. Too often we dwell on past disappointments/delays.

Luke 9:62 reminds us: "But Jesus said to him, 'No one, having put his hand to the plow, and looking back, is fit for the kingdom of God.'"

As Christians, the moment God starts carrying us through the different tests of our faith—loss of finance, loss of friends, betrayal, persecution, isolation, barrenness, time tests, and wilderness experiences, many look back and eventually fall away. Looking back disqualifies us and eliminates us from God's maximum use and robs us of the purpose and plan God has in store for us.

Genesis 19:26 (read the entire scripture) speaks to us about Lot and his wife! Even as God is delivering us from different issues of life and danger, many look back/go back to the things of the past. We must be careful where our affection lies, because that is where our hearts lie also. When we look backward, judgment will engulf us. When God offered Lot security and safety by instructing him to go to the mountain, he wanted more security than he felt the mountain offered. In many respects, he modeled the grip of this present age. The fulfilling and seeking of safety in temporal things are seen in Lot's rapid departure. Many times, God gives us a way of escape—he best way—but many still look back and hold on to the things of the past! They refuse to see the new life that awaits ahead. They would prefer to disobey God, refuse His instructions (like Lot did), and end up in a cave. Disobedience opens the door for many wrong choices and pain. God demanded of them a total abandonment of the condemned city, in heart and will, and their refusal to do so led to Lot's wife's demise!

So it is time for us to declare that "good things are ahead" and move past "the good ol' days."

Do Not Be Afraid to Start Over!

Let us all embrace this time as one of new beginnings! We are in a season where God wants to do something new in the lives of various persons. For many to advance, they will need to start over, and starting over is not something many want to or find easy to do—particularly in relationships, employment, or migration. Some are even going through some difficulties, and God would even want to change their geographic location.

Prosperity, faith, and life are each a journey! Wherever favor no longer exists, then it is time to move to the next location, and by so doing, we will need to start over, and it may bring us back to basics. Going back to basics means we will need to leave some things behind—friends, family, and assets. In other instances, we may need to leave fame and popularity behind to attain the new and greater that lies ahead!

God has a path for us to walk and provision to sustain us as well. Starting over also means going into a new profession or field of study. A person may currently be a politician, but God has a greater purpose. You might be a doctor, but what if God is calling you to work in the mission field? You may be a lawyer, and God is calling you into counseling and teaching to help the upcoming generation, but you become filled with fear. What if God is calling you to raise up a school, university, or a not-for-profit organization?

Your profession for which you have trained is not necessarily your purpose/calling. Purpose is birthed out of pain and passion. What makes you sad is a clue to your purpose or what makes you angry and what makes very happy are clues to your purpose.

Greater Growth

Each of us was created to bear fruit, but not many are wrongly positioned.

Starting over may mean that we will need to make some drastic decisions. For example, you may be in an abusive relationship, but because of the "benefits," you are fearful of leaving. Some may also be in a common-law relationship, and the other party refuses to be married. They allow the fear factor to hinder them from walking in their true potential.

Move by faith by starting over! Money is not all! Even if it means sleeping on the floor for a while, not going to the hairdresser for a while and doing your own hair, skipping the barber's chair for a while, or not eating out as often, it can open the doors for greater possibilities!

Many work in a company for years and have experienced very little growth or success in the organization. But God would want them to step out and start their own business! The fear of failure consumes them. Fear of failure is a condition of the mind, as is poverty! There are even people that God would want to migrate into other countries, but because they are fearful and refuse, they lose their authority and power where they stay.

Are you willing to be demoted for greater promotion? Are you willing to take less pay? Are you willing to take a lower position in an organization for a greater possibility in the future?

Transition

This may bring discomfort and push you out of your comfortability! It may even affect your children for a short while. Politicians themselves who lose an election also have to start over. They go through transitions also, because the daily access they had to certain things they no longer have. But transition is a time of gaining greater wisdom and understanding and opens our eyes to new possibilities. This can also be one of the most difficult times, but this can also draw you closer to God, to seek His face. It is a period that shows you your true friends!

Transition helps you to see things differently—from a different perspective. There are many people who live from paycheck to paycheck, and they don't believe they can live without a salary for even a moment, but during the period of transition, they find themselves living better than they did when they had a salary!

Never be afraid to start over! It can be the greatest period of gain for you!

CHAPTER 35

THE POWER OF FASTING AND IMPORTANCE OF PRAYER

Fasting is one of the most effective tools we have to help us achieve success and true prosperity. It brings solutions, healing, and favor for individuals, nations, and businesses. It also stops judgment on a nation. Once one understands the power and the secret embedded in fasting, then one is already on the right path for success.

Years ago, when I worked at a major organization, it was faced with serious problems, and no one knew what to do. They tried everything and even went as far as inviting expatriates to come and help to solve the problem. A number of jobs were about to be cut as a way of cutting down operational expenses, but no solutions were forthcoming. The staff members were instructed to go on a fast. When they did that, immediately, transformation took place! The solutions came in abundance, and numerous jobs were saved! There was a huge turnaround within the organization—the fast had brought about tremendous change. The organization at that time became a model for other companies! Even the trade unions were surprised!

Divine Intervention

Can you imagine if the leader of this nation decided to stand up one day and call the other political parties, the public and private sector leaders together, and say, "Let us put our political issues aside and cry out to the Lord for solutions and for divine intervention in this nation"? There would be changes in the economy, the killing of children would cease, the corruption would decrease significantly, and there would be solutions and favor upon the nation!

Kinds of Fasts

Now, there are different kinds of fasts, and a fast can range from one to forty days.

With all these fasts, there are different levels, which include partial, absolute, juice, and vegetables fasts. Before you fast, check with your physician, and once you have been deemed healthy enough to fast, wash your face, anoint your head, and go on the fast.

Fasting has been tested and proven! Many persons—whether religious—know that fasting is a tested and proven tool and that it never fails to accomplish the goal!

Some examples of fasts include the following:

One-day Fast: To hear from God and for spiritual examination is found in Genesis 23:27 and Judges 20:18.

One-day Ezra Fast: For guidance and protection for our children and security for our possession and our businesses is found in Ezra 8:21–23. (This fast will bring God's protection and cut down on crime.)

One-day Daniel Night Fast: For national leaders dealing with a life-threatening situation in their administration is found in Daniel 6:18.

One-day Joel 2 Fast: For the turnaround in a nation's economy, to avert judgment, break famine, cut crime, and bring new business ideas and improvement to the agricultural sector is found in Joel 2.

One-day Samuel Fast: For religious leaders to bring victory over the enemy and purge the nation of images and idols is found in 1 Samuel 7:1–12.

One-day Isaiah 58 Fast: To break yokes, for peace and inner-city renewal, and to restore the value of real estate is found in Isaiah 58.

One-day Jonah Fast: To avert disasters (earthquakes, tsunamis, and tidal waves) is found in Jonah 3:5–9

Three-day Fast: This brings favor, healing, and breakthrough, opens doors, and gives God's favor in legal issues is found in 1 Samuel 30:11–20 and Esther 4.

Seven-day Consecration Fast: Brings us into the presence of the Lord and gives us God's favor is found in Ezekiel 43:35–37.

Ten-day Daniel Fast: Brings healing, divine revelation, and Godly wisdom, and deals with witchcraft is found in Daniel 1.

Twenty-one-day Daniel Fast: Brings fresh revelation and solutions, breaks down strongholds over individuals and nations, and releases God's angels over the nation is found in Daniel 10.

Fast for Your Harvest!

Undoubtedly, this season is one of blessing for the faithful in Christ, and we will see the blessings of the Lord unfold as never before! God is also about to give us rest from the things of the past, from enemies, whether the enemy is emotional, financial, or otherwise. God wants to put an end to something in your life that has been holding you back from receiving the fullness of His blessing for you. All He wants is our obedience, and what would take seven years to accomplish, He will accomplish in seven days.

God wants to restore His people and to pour new wine in you and heal your broken heart! He wants those who are abused to receive His healing. He wants to restore the poor, the fatherless, and the widow; He wants to restore those who have been forgotten and to lift them up. This is the season in which you should seek Him like never before! Get deeper in Him and repent of the things that we do and say that hinder us so that the times of refreshing will come and that God will restore all things.

Get everything you need together and start that business now! Despite the academic or financial setbacks you may have, start school now! Step out by faith and go for that dream house now! Extend your faith so that God may enlarge your territory and extend your borders! We have entered a season of *harvest*! Don't be left out!

This is the instruction of the Lord for this season! Go on a twenty-one-day fast according to Daniel 10:13. Eat only vegetables and water (no sweet things). While on this fast, declare Psalm 21 over your life daily! Write down twenty-one things for which you are believing the Lord in this season. Send a copy of that list to us at rwominc@yahoo.com as well as a seed/donation into our RWOMI Humanitarian Outreach of as little as twenty-one dollars through www.rwominc.com, and we will join with you to pray over them.

You can fast from midnight to 1:00 p.m. or 3:00 p.m. the following day. For those with serious health issues, you can fast for three hours! Everyone on this twenty-one-day fast should follow this instruction. Each day for the twenty-one days, select and pray for one of the items on your list. For example:

- Day 1 Physical Healing
- Day 2 A New Job
- Day 3 Restoration of My Family
- Day 4 A New Anointing
- Day 5 For Victory With The Immigration Issues

and so on. By doing this, you will hear His voice clearly, and God will

- give you guidance;
- give you new revelations and business ideas;
- show you things to come; or
- give you financial breakthrough.

The key to our deliverance and breakthrough is obedience to the prophetic instruction, according to Deuteronomy 28. Only through Divine revelation from God will you be set free!

Prayer Breaks Recession

Prayer is not a word that many like to hear, particularly in connection with the economy, financial systems, and technology. However, it is interesting to note that prayer is the first wireless communication and has been around since the dawn of time. Furthermore, it has always been free, and the only way it is ineffective is when it is not done with a pure heart.

Prayer involves intercession, thanksgiving, and petitioning. Petitioning is a formal application or entreaty to an authority. It is also a written action by a government signed by a number of people.

God is the ultimate authority and the final government. Imagine what would happen if all the stakeholders in a nation came together petitioning God to bring change within the nations and even the global economy, and that righteous governance come into effect; change would take place worldwide.

The day any government, prime minister, president, or monarch ignores criticism and ridicule and calls their nation to one day of prayer for the Lord to intervene in the affairs of the nation, we would be surprised to see the solutions and the change that would come forth.

There is always such a fight against prayer. But if prayer is such a bad thing, then why ask for it during times of adversity?

Take note that prayer is extremely effective—so much so that it can break recession, change the economy, and bring spiritual and natural revival, growth, and prosperity to a nation (1 Kings 18; Joel 1–2).

Persistence in prayer deals with injustice, disaster, evil, poverty, and war (Luke 18:1–8).

The number-one priority in church, nation, or business must be prayer—then the nation would have peace. The first wall of defense in a nation must be prayer, not weaponry and the national security forces, unless the Lord builds the house we labor in vain! (Psalm 127:1–2).

When the wall of prayer breaks down within a nation, the following will occur (Ezekiel 13:5; Ezekiel 22:30):

1) family divisions
2) internal and external security issues
3) governmental problems

4)   false doctrines, false teachers, and powerlessness in church
5)   attraction of the wrong advisers to the government
6)   lack of new ideas and investment
7)   shift in the motives of those in the media
8)   wrong kind of educators entering the education system

When the wall of prayer is torn down, then we have famine, recession, violence, corruption, evil, and great poverty.

The Power of Prayer

Matthew 6:9–13 tells us that prayer reduces debt, gives daily provision, brings God's will to pass, and causes what takes place in the heavens to also take place on the earth. Prayer gives us natural and spiritual sustenance and power, and protects us from evil.

According to Luke 21–22 and 1 Kings 18:36–46, prayer opens the heavens (and the world needs an open heaven right now). An open heaven means that healing, solutions, changes, and strengthening will take place. Recognize also that

a)   prayer changes God's heart (2 Kings 20:1–7) and brings healing. Prayer caused God to add fifteen years to a king's life after he had decided to take his life away.
b)   prayer delivers a nation in times of war and gives it victory and allows the nation to collect the spoils (2 Chronicles 20:1–13).

It is noteworthy that in 1 Timothy 2:8, God outlines that man should pray everywhere—nowhere is exempt. When this happens, then we will see a global change in businesses, various organizations, and in individuals' lives and homes.

Additionally, prayer allows us to be bold; it breaks plots and gives you victory over your enemies (Ephesians 6:18–20; Proverbs 6:7–10; Psalm 109:4).

Those that are going through hardship will be wiser in their prayer. The more difficult times become, the more people will pray. The more people pray, the stronger they become and the better able they are to handle their problems.

Daily Prayer for Provision to Come to Your Door

Always pray for daily deals, discounts, favor, debt write-offs and debt cancellation, checks in the mail, opportunities, sales, gold, silver, cash, daily revelation and anointing, open vision, dreams, documents to be signed in your favor, promotion, protection from cyber threats, shame and disgrace, accidents and incidents, health, strength, and increase in discernment.

Prayer

Father, in the name of Jesus, I pray for the manifestation of Your blessings will find my address—daily deals, discounts, favor, debt write-offs and debt cancellation, checks in the mail, opportunities, sales, gold, silver, cash, daily revelation and anointing, open vision, dreams, documents to be signed in my favor, promotion, protection from cyber threats, shame and disgrace, accidents and incidents, health, strength and increase in discernment. Lord, I thank You that You have already done it. Let there be fresh impartation each day from the Holy Spirit. I thank You for giving to my family and to me land for which we did not labor and cities that we did not build, and we shall dwell in them; we will eat of the vineyards and olive groves that we did not plant.

Prayer for the Spirit of Wisdom
(Ephesians 1:15–23; Ephesians 3:14–21)

To be an effective servant of God, we need the Spirit of Wisdom and Revelation in the knowledge of Him; not only Christians but also all global leaders and their families. Most are falling because of a lack of knowledge. Having true knowledge and wisdom first begins with God.

Many have knowledge and wisdom but not from the Holy Spirit of God, and as a result, there is chaos and failure.

We see in the book of Daniel that God gives revelation to empower for problem-solving and healing. The question we have to ask is, what knowledge and source of wisdom are we employing on a daily basis? Only God can reveal the hope of His calling to us and the riches of the glory of His inheritance in His saints according to the working of His mighty power.

We must pray for the Holy Spirit to fill every believer. We must pray to become mighty by His power. We must pray to be rooted and grounded in Him like a tree in the love of Christ and grounded like a building on a strong foundation. We must pray to receive His fullness, truth, and power as well as His blessings and His wisdom (Zechariah 8:18–23; 2 Thessalonians 3:1–5).

CHAPTER 36

YOU CAN MAKE IT
IN HARD TIMES

Many are now crumbling under these hard times. Some are giving up, and others are even taking their own lives! People are now realizing that politicians are not representing the interests of the people they supposedly represent but, instead, their own interests! But, regardless of how hard it is, each person must know that he/she can make it. It really depends on a person's daily personal choices. Each day, God creates opportunities and access to blessings (Psalm 68:19). The bad economy has nothing to do with one's daily survival. You can get blessed in any season (Psalm 68:9).

We must begin to embrace the fact that the politicians don't determine your future—you do! They are not responsible for your children's not going to school; neither are they responsible for the poor choices you may make—adulterous relationships, common-law relationships, producing children you refuse to take care of, and spreading HIV and other sexually transmitted diseases. It is a waste of precious time and much energy to become bitter with family members (particularly those overseas) who can't help you on a regular basis.

Even if you are/were a school dropout, for whatever reason, you can still rise out of your present situation. Don't blame yourself and dwell on past mistakes; think about your future and rise like a phoenix. Most of us are allowing our past to determine and even be our future. God made us with many gifts, talents, and ideas to rise out of our present situation. There is always something in our midst during the hard times to bring us out of poverty, debt, and hopelessness! (2 Kings 4:1–7).

Many are looking for the easy way out, so they get involved in "drug transportation," illegal weapons possession, and other criminal activities. Many involved in these activities are being used by rich individuals who don't have the desire to go the straight and narrow way and don't care about whom they use. Ask the question: how many "big men" do you see going to prison? Even if you are fatherless, it is no excuse for getting involved in crime for survival! There are many persons who were without a father in their lives, but they made it big. Persons such as Rex Nettleford, Gordon "Butch" Stewart, the Matalons, the Issas, William "Bill" Cosby, Dr. Benjamin "Ben" Carson—they all started from poor backgrounds; some without fathers present, and their names are known today.

Don't Sell Yourself

- You are more valuable than an iPad, Blackberry, Android, or any amount of cash! Don't allow yourself to be used sexually to get these things.
- Seek for an education! You have the capacity to own businesses while you maintain your moral values!
- Be wise! Keep away from brand names; most of these business moguls have made it already—*you* can make it too! Why would you spend three or four times the money to get brand name items when you could invest that in your education or in your own family for a better tomorrow!
- Dress simply!
- You don't need to drive in luxury-priced vehicles when you can get something less costly and save.

- Don't sell yourselves to get rich.

Some of the greatest things you can have are good health, a solid education, a debt-free home, and a family. One of life's greatest rewards is having the ability to help humanity!

Back to Basics

In hard times, for survival, it is cheaper and healthier to make use of the things that God has placed in our surroundings or environment. For example, it is cheaper and healthier to drink lime and water or the basic lemonade than it is to guzzle processed drinks. Limes and lemons have ten times the health benefits of the processed drinks and "juices."

It is healthier and less expensive to grill or bake your meats than it is to microwave the processed foods. Not only does it damage your health but also it pushes up your electricity bill significantly. The good old wood or coal fires are better for our health. I am sure that there is someone who can come up with good ideas to make that work despite today's fast-paced global existence. Where there is natural spring water, cut down on importing water and source your own! Boil and purify your water and stop spending so much on imports!

Finally, when God gives you dreams and visions, it is to help you to be a better person. Stop gambling your life away! Find some people less fortunate than yourself and give what you were planning to gamble and see what a difference it will make to them and for you.

The Problem with Problems

We are in a critical period where there are problems in every direction—health, family, economic, sexual, and numerous other problems, all stress related. Even suicide has increased dramatically. Problems, problems everywhere!

Problems are gates to change. When a problem arises, it is an opportunity for change, and it has the potential to give you solutions and bring out new ideas, wisdom, and hidden gifts. Problems have the potential to increase your general capacity for problem-solving. They allow us to dig deeper, spiritually speaking, and increase our trust in God. Oftentimes, however, the problem is not really the problem. The problem with problems lies in how we deal with our problems.

Problems can create new relationships (1 Samuel 17:57–58), and there is always something within your surroundings—regardless of how small it may be—that can help you out of your problems. In 2 Kings 4, the creditors were coming to collect from the widow. But because she followed God's instructions, the small bottle of oil she had causes her to move from total indebtedness to total debt freedom. There is something that you have that can take you out of your situation—out of poverty—and cause you to become a major shareholder!

Without problems to solve, you would not have a salary. Certain professions would not exist. People excel when they solve problems. What sometimes seems like a major problem is oftentimes what God uses to promote you. The more problems exist, the greater the needs are for solutions. Solutions take us out of poverty.

Further to all this, problems develop your leadership skills and expose those around you with wrong motives. When problems cease to exist, your services are no longer required.

Interestingly, credit unions have always made efforts to solve problems for the poor. So any administration that chooses to put unfair measures in place in the credit unions is creating more economic problems that the nation and the administration can do without.

Now, not to be forgotten is the fact that some people will create problems to bring their solutions with hidden motives. We need some people who are willing to solve problems they did not create.

Dealing with Problems

When problems arise:

- Recognize and accept that the problem that you face is a clue to the problems you were created to solve.

- Begin to look around your life, your community, and your nation and look at the problems that exist and then begin to dig deep for the solutions.
- Remember that the reward you decide to receive determines the problem you decide to solve. For example, David rose to power because there were political and economic problems. The politicians in those days did not know how to deal with giants.
- Use them as a stepping-stone for change and promotion rather than allowing it to overwhelm you. Always have a positive attitude when problems arise and use it as a golden connection and for networking.
- Remember, solving problems opens doors to uncommon leaders (Daniel 1:19–20), and it also determines the quality of leaders that pursue you.
- Cast them to Jesus, and He will take it and give you the solutions (1 Peter 5:7).
- Never try to solve your problems with alcohol, drugs, adultery, gambling, crime, or promiscuity—these are not problem solvers; they are problem makers.

Faith and trust in God and a wholehearted acceptance of His principles can solve most, if not all, of your problems.

Problems create new jobs. For example, when there is a natural disaster, the need arises for more construction workers, more laborers, increased police presence, and more food distribution and manufacturing activities, and more personnel. You will also need more counselors and liaisons to gather, collate, and disseminate information to make good decisions that will benefit all involved.

The Next Big Problem

The next big problem we are about to see is the environmental problem, contamination of food, toxic substances that have been and continue to be released in the earth, and so on. Are we ready to solve these problems?

Every Problem Has an Expiration Date

There are many going through hardships and facing problems from every direction. Many ask the question, "Why am I going through all this?" We often go through problems but recognize that it pulls out of us the hidden potential we didn't realize was within us. We go through problems and testing, but these experiences can help to strengthen us and allow us to help others.

Oftentimes, we don't even remember God and His goodness until we are going through times of great difficulty. Many going through difficulty are giving up, and some are even committing suicide. Regardless of how big your problem may seem, recognize that every problem has an expiration date. Your date can be today!

When you are going through problems, always focus on the problems from which the Lord has already delivered you! They are no longer problems but victories! Remember the goodness and grace of God Who brought you through those problems! If He has delivered you from the problems before, will He not do it again?

Many times, the problems we go through are based on our purpose, our assignment, and the vow(s) we have made. Sometimes people become comfortable and don't remember where they are coming from, and God is trying to get our attention. Just remember, when going through the problems, don't focus on the problem; instead, focus on the victory! When we focus on the problem, the mountain becomes greater.

There is always a solution within the problems, and, sometimes, that solution is what will allow you to become greater! Speak to your problems daily. Speak positive words and outcomes. For example, thank God for the victory you anticipate! Always find scriptural basis to deal with the problem. So if it is a sickness you are facing, then declare Isaiah 53:5. If you are going through bankruptcy or serious financial woes, then declare Psalm 112. If a door has been closed to you and you don't know how to proceed, then declare Isaiah 43:16.

Make and spend time with God and tell Him about the problems. Problems are a sign that God wants to get your attention. We are often too busy trying to do everything to survive when God says we should seek Him first!

Maintaining a relationship with God is the key to success. Most countries and organizations are now failing. They have nothing new to download or to offer because they are spiritually bankrupt!

Many times we pray for promotion and blessing, but God wants depth! There are too many people in this world that have height without depth, and that's why there is a great falling!

Remember, as 2 Corinthians 4:16–18 reminds us: "Therefore we do not lose heart. Even though our outward man is perishing, yet the inward man is being renewed day by day. For our light affliction, which is but for a moment, is working for us a far more exceeding and eternal weight of glory, while we do not look at the things which are seen, but at the things which are not seen. For the things which are seen are temporary, but the things which are not seen are eternal." All we are going through is temporary! Our mind is being renewed, and our inner man is being strengthened. Many times people say they can't live without another paycheck, but they must remember that God is their first source, and God can allow you to live without a paycheck and live better than before.

Problems are the gates for change. Job only realized who his true friends were in his time of great adversity. He was going through the problems, not because he was cursed but because God was proving who was around him and Who was with him.

One of people's biggest fears in life is to lose things—your job, friends, family, status, and position. Sometimes you don't even know who you really are until you lose something or someone close to you!

Remember, an eagle does not learn how to fly until the mother stirs up the nest and even forces it out! The unjust servant did not know how good a negotiator and salesperson he was until the boss planned to fire him! Sometimes, a person never knows who his/her Boaz or Ruth is until he/she gets kicked out or hurt in a relationship!

Don't commit suicide in the midst of the problem; it doesn't solve the problem! You are using a permanent action for a temporary problem. Walk through it—you will come out! Greater is always ahead of you!

CHAPTER 37

GOD'S BLESSINGS ON THE FAMILY

God's blessings on the family is critical. There are many within the legal system now that are attempting to change definitions regarding the family. We must recognize that whatever God does not bless cannot be recognized. When the legal system tries to recognize what God does not sanction, it will not work. Only what God created can be fruitful and multiply. The entire host of heaven sanctioned the creation of the human race. Adam is one of the four Hebrew words for "man." God's plan is to reveal Himself in the earth through man.

When God said, "Let Us make man in Our own image" (Genesis 1:26), God was speaking about qualities, personality, intellect, and the capacity to hear, see, and speak. Man must therefore walk in holiness, truth, righteousness, light, and love, and we must love the things God loves and hate the things He hates. We were created to be Kingdom agents planting holy seeds through procreation and commanded to train that seed in God's ways.

The legal system has been trying to redefine family, but all that has done and will continue to do is cause chaos and problems both spiritually and naturally. Man should never try to go below the value of what God created them to be.

When man fails to walk in their God-given dominion, it reduces their power and influence in the earth. We were created for one thing, and that is to worship God only.

From Creation, Satan's main goal is for man to gain spiritual knowledge illegally, wanting us to focus on the material things of life while ignoring the correct spiritual things. He wants man to walk in falsehood where he is worshipped, but worship belongs only to God.

Today, many families are breaking up while they ignore the Holy Spirit, not realizing that the blessings come from God, and as His Word says, "The blessing of the Lord makes one rich, and He adds no sorrow with it" (Proverbs 10:22).

It is time for man to get back to the Creator and lay hold of the His blessings according to His plans and purpose for our lives—the life He gave to each of us. I have spoken to many successful people, and one of the greatest pains they have experienced is that after achieving all they did, most of them have lost their families. As soon as prosperity increased, one spouse turned away from the other. There are even situations where fathers have never spent a Christmas, birthday, or even Thanksgiving with their families.

The governments, lobbyists, and groups with other agendas have been shifting the focus to many other causes and reasons for the state of the world being as it is when the fact is that everything broken in the society, economy, church, government, legal system, business sector, and any other facet within the nations is the result of the brokenness within the family.

It is time for us to refocus and get back to basics so that the healing of the family and, ultimately, the nation can begin.

BIBLIOGRAPHY

Hagee, John C., executive editor. *Prophecy Study Bible*. New King James Version. Copyright © 1997.

Hayford, Jack W., executive editor, *New Spirit-Filled Life® Bible*. New King James Version. Copyright © 2002 Thomas Nelson Inc.

Swaggart, Jimmy. *The Holy Bible. The Expositor's Study Bible*. King James Version. Copyright © 2008, Jimmy Swaggart Ministries. Baton Rouge, Louisiana.

Lyston, Steve. *Man, Money, Ministry*. Xlibris Corporation. Copyright © 2009. All Rights Reserved.

Pfeiffer, Charles F., Howard F. Vos, and John Rea, editors. *Wycliffe Bible Dictionary*, (Seventh Printing). Copyright © 2005 Hendrickson Publishers Inc.

http://www.abort73.com/print/460/

https://www.biblegateway.com/resources/dictionary-of-bible-themes/5654-betrothal

http://jamaica-gleaner.com/gleaner/20121115/lead/lead3.html

https://macaulay.cuny.edu/eportfolios/libertylinks/2013/03/25/
what-the-founding-fathers-said-about-the-second-amendment/

http://www.notablebiographies.com/He-Ho/Honda-Soichiro.html

http://www.pcuc.org/statistics-on-abortion/

ABOUT THE AUTHOR

Apostle Dr. Steve Lyston is the author of several solutions-oriented books – End-Time Finance, The New Millionaire, Man Money Ministry, Prayer Works and Tactics and Strategies for the Famine. Apostle Dr. Steve Lyston has been in Ministry for almost 20 years having done another 20 years prior in the armed forces and the secular management field. He is an ordained Bishop over several churches in the USA, the Caribbean, South America, India and Africa. He is the Apostle of Restoration World Outreach Ministries Incorporated, Restoration Outreach Ministries International and of Lyston Consultancy & Enterprises LLC. He regularly writes for the Jamaica Gleaner and other online media houses. He has been n apostolic, prophetic voice over the years particularly regarding Biblical Economics with an insatiable passion for helping the poor. He advises several government and business leaders. He also has an online video publication called Revelation Time. He is married with 3 children.

To invite Apostle Dr. Steve and Pastor Dr. Michelle Lyston for a speaking engagement, please contact through

www.lystonvoice.com
www.rwominc.com
www.rwominetwork.com

E-mail us at biblical_economics@yahoo.com or
rwominc@yahoo.com